Fine Fitness: Achieve Peak Performance Through Exercise, Nutrition and Mindful Movement

PUBLISHED BY Alexandra Brennan

© **Copyright 2025 - All rights reserved.**

All introductions, analyses, and commentaries contained within this book may not be reproduced, duplicated, or transmitted without direct written permission from the author or the publisher. Under no circumstances will any blame or legal responsibility be held against the publisher or author for any damages, reparation, or monetary loss due to the information contained within this book, either directly or indirectly.

Legal Notice:

This book is only for personal use. You cannot amend, distribute, sell, use, quote, or paraphrase any part of the introductions, analyses, or commentaries within this book, without the consent of the author or publisher.

Disclaimer Notice:

Please note the information contained within this document is for educational and entertainment purposes only. All efforts have been executed to present accurate, up-to-date, reliable, complete information. No warranties of any kind are declared or implied. Readers acknowledge that the author is not engaged in the rendering of legal, financial, medical, or professional advice. The content within this book has been derived from various sources. Please consult a licensed professional before attempting any techniques outlined in this book.

By reading this document, the reader agrees that under no circumstances is the author responsible for any losses, direct or indirect, that are incurred as a result of the use of the information contained within this document, including, but not limited to, errors, omissions, or inaccuracies.

Table of contents

Introduction — The Convergence of Body, Fuel, and Flow 4

Chapter 1: The Adaptive Body — Understanding Your Biological Blueprint for Transformation 10

Chapter 2: Metabolic Flexibility — Engineering Your Energy Systems 22

Chapter 3: The Architecture of Movement — Building Functional Strength Through Pattern Mastery 33

Chapter 4: The Nutrition Matrix — Precision Fueling for Performance 43

Chapter 5: Recovery Architecture — The Science of Supercompensation 53

Chapter 6: Mindful Movement Mastery — The Consciousness-Performance Connection 64

Chapter 7: The Hormonal Optimization Blueprint 75

Chapter 8: Advanced Training Periodization — The Art of Strategic Programming 85

Chapter 9: Environmental Training Optimization 95

Chapter 10: The Integration Protocol — Creating Your Personal Performance System 105

Conclusion — The Harmony of Body, Fuel, and Flow 114

Introduction — The Convergence of Body, Fuel, and Flow

In every generation, people search for the secret to unlocking their greatest potential. Some turn to extreme diets, others to grueling training regimens, while many hope for a breakthrough supplement or a technological shortcut. Yet beneath all the noise, the truth remains both simple and profound: the human body was designed not just to survive, but to thrive in a state where movement, nourishment, and inner focus converge into a seamless whole. This integration—where body, fuel, and flow intersect—creates the foundation of what we call *fine fitness*.

Fine fitness is not about chasing a fleeting aesthetic ideal or exhausting oneself in endless cycles of punishment and reward. It is not the frantic pursuit of burning calories for the sake of erasure, nor is it the obsessive measuring of macronutrients without understanding their harmony. At its core, fine fitness is about cultivating a relationship with the body that honors its design, fuels its processes with intelligence, and taps into the mental state that transforms effort into mastery. It is where physiology meets psychology, where science blends with lived experience, and where performance ceases to be mechanical and begins to feel like art.

To understand this convergence, we must first dismantle the cultural silos that have kept training, nutrition, and mental focus separate. In the modern world, fitness is often approached in fragmented compartments: the gym as one space, the kitchen as another, and mindfulness relegated to a distant corner reserved for yogis or meditators. Yet in truth, these dimensions are inseparable. A body trained without nourishment becomes brittle; nourishment consumed without movement becomes stagnant; focus pursued without physical vitality remains abstract. It is only when the three pillars align that fitness transcends into something sustainable, resilient, and transformative.

The body, at its most basic level, is a marvel of engineering. Muscles contract through orchestrated electrical signals, bones bear loads with architectural brilliance, and the cardiovascular system delivers oxygen with relentless precision. But unlike a machine, the body is adaptive. Every stressor, from lifting a heavy weight to running a mile or even mastering a complex dance sequence, leaves behind a trace—an imprint on the nervous system, muscles, and cellular metabolism. Over time, these imprints accumulate, reshaping the body into what it practices most. This adaptability is both a gift and a responsibility. The gift lies in the possibility of transformation; the responsibility lies in choosing what we adapt to. A lifestyle of inactivity and processed foods also reshapes the body, but into fragility and disease. Fine fitness asks us to take ownership of this adaptability and direct it consciously.

Fuel, in this equation, is far more than calories or grams of protein. It is the chemistry of vitality. Every cell in the human body relies on precise molecular transactions powered by nutrients that come from what we eat and drink. The mitochondria in our muscles and organs do not distinguish between the calories of a doughnut and the calories of fresh fruit, yet the accompanying micronutrients—or lack thereof—determine whether those calories build resilience or decay. Nutrition, when approached as fuel rather than indulgence or punishment, becomes an act of empowerment. It is a way to prime the body for performance, recovery, and long-term health. Fine fitness reframes food not as the enemy to be restricted or the indulgence to be excused, but as the cornerstone of cellular excellence.

The third element—flow—is the most elusive, yet perhaps the most transformative. Flow is the state of complete immersion in activity where time seems to dissolve and effort becomes effortless. Athletes describe it as "being in the zone," musicians as being carried by rhythm, and meditators as dissolving into pure presence. From a scientific standpoint, flow is a state of neurochemical optimization: dopamine, norepinephrine, and endorphins align to sharpen focus, elevate mood, and reduce the perception of pain. In the context of fine fitness, flow bridges the gap between discipline and joy. It transforms a workout from a task into a ritual, nutrition from a restriction into a celebration, and self-care from obligation into expression. Without flow, fitness becomes drudgery; with flow, it becomes an enduring part of life's rhythm.

When body, fuel, and flow operate in isolation, their impact is limited. A person may train relentlessly but undermine progress with poor nutrition. Another may eat flawlessly but lack the stimulus of movement to direct those nutrients toward strength and resilience. Others may meditate deeply but neglect the physical vessel that supports the mind. But when these three forces converge, their effects amplify one another in ways that cannot be achieved through partial effort. A nourished body recovers faster and trains harder. A focused mind sustains consistency and resists burnout. A strong body provides the physiological foundation for mental clarity and emotional stability. Together, they create a cycle of reinforcement that elevates performance, health, and quality of life.

This book, *Fine Fitness: The Convergence of Body, Fuel, and Flow*, was born from the recognition that fragmented approaches to wellness no longer suffice in a world where demands on the human body and mind are unprecedented. We live in an era where many people sit for hours each day, scrolling through information, yet simultaneously crave vitality, presence, and resilience. Quick fixes abound—detox teas, extreme diets, miracle machines—but none address the integrated reality of human performance. The purpose of this work is to restore that integration, to show how the body's design, the fuel it requires, and the flow state it can achieve are not separate disciplines but parts of a single whole.

Fine fitness is also about redefining success. Traditional fitness culture often measures progress in visible metrics: pounds lifted, miles run, inches lost. While these markers can be motivating, they risk reducing a deeply human journey into a checklist. Fine fitness measures success by quality: quality of movement, quality of energy, and quality of presence. It is not about how much you can punish your body, but how well you can align with its potential. It asks whether your training enhances your life outside the gym, whether your nutrition fuels not only performance but clarity and mood, and whether your pursuit of fitness brings you closer to yourself rather than alienating you from your own body.

Consider, for a moment, an elite dancer performing on stage. The audience sees grace, power, and expression. Behind the scenes, that performance is made possible by relentless training of the body, precise fueling through nutrition, and an unwavering immersion in flow. Strip away any one of those elements and the performance falters. A malnourished dancer lacks endurance. A distracted mind breaks rhythm. An untrained body cannot express what the mind envisions. Now consider that the same principles apply to everyday life. Whether one is preparing for a demanding work project, parenting with energy and patience, or simply wanting to walk into a room with confidence, the same convergence determines the outcome. Fine fitness is not only for athletes—it is for anyone seeking to live fully.

Another aspect that distinguishes fine fitness is sustainability. Fads may deliver short-term results but leave behind exhaustion or metabolic damage. Fine fitness is not a sprint toward a narrow goal but a lifelong journey toward vitality. It values consistency over extremity, adaptability over rigidity. Just as ecosystems thrive through balance, the human body thrives when exercise, nutrition, and mental focus are balanced rather than pushed to extremes. This sustainability ensures that fitness enhances life rather than dominates it, that discipline becomes devotion rather than obsession.

As you embark on this journey through the chapters ahead, you will discover how the body can be trained to unlock its latent power, how fuel can be optimized to support both physical and mental performance, and how flow can be cultivated to make the entire process not only effective but deeply fulfilling. You will learn how science and experience intertwine, how ancient wisdom and modern research complement one another, and how small daily practices create compounding transformations. The ultimate goal is not to offer another rigid program but to illuminate a path where the integration of body, fuel, and flow becomes second nature—where fitness is not something you do, but something you live.

Fine fitness, then, is not merely a concept but an invitation. It invites you to see your body not as a problem to be solved but as an ally to be honored. It invites you to treat food not as a battleground but as a source of power. It invites you to enter flow not as a rare accident but as a trainable state. And most of all, it invites you to converge these forces so that your potential is not left scattered across disconnected practices but united in a whole that is greater than the sum of its parts.

In a world that often urges us to compartmentalize, fine fitness insists on integration. And in that integration lies not only the key to health and performance but the art of living itself.

Chapter 1: The Adaptive Body — Understanding Your Biological Blueprint for Transformation

"The human body can produce enough heat in 30 minutes to boil half a gallon of water, yet 95% of people never tap into more than 20% of their physical potential."

1.1 Decoding Your Genetic Athletic Profile

Every human body carries within it a unique code—an intricate script written in DNA—that shapes how it responds to training, how quickly it recovers, and what kind of performance it is naturally inclined toward. This code is not a fixed sentence but rather a set of possibilities, a blueprint with room for interpretation. The field of modern fitness often treats the body as a universal machine, prescribing identical routines and expecting identical outcomes, yet the truth is that no two people adapt in the same way. Understanding your genetic athletic profile is the first step in working with your body rather than against it, tailoring training and recovery to align with its natural predispositions.

One of the most fundamental distinctions in this profile is muscle fiber composition. Human skeletal muscles are not uniform; they are made up of fibers that fall broadly into two categories: slow-twitch (Type I) and fast-twitch (Type II). Slow-twitch fibers are fatigue-resistant, designed for endurance activities such as long-distance running, cycling, or swimming. They generate less force but can sustain effort for extended periods because they are rich in mitochondria and rely primarily on aerobic metabolism. Fast-twitch fibers, by contrast, are built for explosive power. They fire rapidly, contract with greater force, and are fueled largely by anaerobic processes, making them ideal for sprinting, jumping, or heavy lifting, though they fatigue more quickly.

The ratio of these fibers varies significantly from person to person, determined partly by genetics and partly by training. An elite marathoner may have as much as 80% slow-twitch fibers in their leg muscles, while a world-class sprinter may possess the opposite composition, with a dominance of fast-twitch fibers. For the average person, the split hovers closer to an even balance, but small differences can explain why some individuals thrive in endurance pursuits while others excel in short bursts of intensity. Importantly, muscle fibers also show remarkable adaptability. While genetics may tilt the starting point, training stimuli can shift fibers toward characteristics needed for the demands placed upon them. A powerlifter who trains repeatedly in the heavy, explosive range can convert intermediate fibers toward fast-twitch dominance, while an endurance athlete may coax fibers toward greater fatigue resistance.

Identifying your own fiber composition does not require a biopsy or laboratory testing. Observation of movement patterns and recovery rates provides powerful clues. For example, if you find yourself excelling in sprints or feeling naturally powerful in short, intense bursts, it suggests a higher proportion of fast-twitch fibers. Conversely, if you can sustain long runs or high-repetition workouts with less fatigue, slow-twitch fibers may be more prominent. Recovery speed offers another window: those with fast-twitch dominance often need longer rest periods after heavy exertion, while endurance-leaning individuals may recover more rapidly between sessions. This awareness allows you to tailor training intelligently—choosing the balance of volume, intensity, and rest that matches your inherent strengths while still developing weaker areas for well-rounded fitness.

Beyond fiber composition, another layer of genetic athletic profiling lies in epigenetics—the science of how lifestyle and training can influence the expression of genes. While DNA provides the blueprint, epigenetic "switches" determine which parts of the blueprint are activated at any given time. Environmental inputs such as nutrition, exercise, stress, and even sleep can turn genes on or off, amplifying or silencing their influence. This is why two individuals with nearly identical genetic potential can display vastly different outcomes depending on how they live.

Training itself is one of the most potent epigenetic triggers. When you subject your muscles to mechanical stress, biochemical pathways are activated that signal genes to promote growth, repair, and adaptation. Endurance training stimulates genes linked to mitochondrial biogenesis, effectively teaching cells to produce more energy. Strength training, on the other hand, activates genes involved in protein synthesis and neuromuscular recruitment, building denser, more powerful muscle fibers. Over time, these changes become engrained not just in the muscles but in the cellular memory, making the body more efficient at responding to similar stimuli in the future. In this sense, training is not simply about practicing movements; it is about rewriting the operating manual of your body at the molecular level.

Even dormant athletic genes can be awakened through the right kind of stress. For instance, certain pathways linked to growth factors or oxygen utilization remain underutilized until the body is pushed into unfamiliar territory. This is why progressive overload—the gradual increase of training demands—is so effective. By continually nudging the body beyond its comfort zone, you trigger genetic expressions that expand capacity. Epigenetics reminds us that our limits are not carved in stone but are malleable, waiting for the right stimulus to unlock hidden potential.

Layered onto genetics and epigenetics is another dimension often overlooked in training: chronobiology, the study of how biological rhythms influence performance. The human body operates on a circadian rhythm, a roughly 24-hour cycle that regulates hormones, body temperature, and energy availability. These rhythms profoundly affect when we are most primed for different kinds of exertion. For instance, muscle strength and power tend to peak in the late afternoon, when body temperature and neuromuscular coordination are highest. Endurance capacity, however, may align better with morning hours when cortisol levels support sustained energy output.

Understanding your chronobiological profile means paying attention to when you feel most energized and when you experience dips. Some people naturally wake with vigor, ready to train at dawn, while others need hours before their nervous system feels primed. Forcing training against your rhythm often leads to suboptimal results and greater fatigue, while aligning workouts with natural peaks enhances efficiency and reduces injury risk. This does not mean one must rigidly adhere to a schedule dictated by biology; rather, it is about harmonizing training with the body's innate tempo. Even small adjustments—such as timing heavy lifts for the afternoon or planning long runs during a personal energy peak—can dramatically improve performance and recovery.

When fiber composition, epigenetic potential, and chronobiology are considered together, a more complete picture of your athletic blueprint emerges. You begin to understand not only what your body is predisposed to but also how it can be guided, adapted, and optimized. This awareness shifts the mindset from frustration over perceived limitations to curiosity about possibilities. Instead of lamenting a lack of "natural talent," you begin to see that talent itself is fluid—partially gifted but largely cultivated through choices and alignment with your biology.

The most successful athletes, whether knowingly or intuitively, operate in this convergence. They recognize their strengths, train their weaknesses, respect their rhythms, and leverage the science of adaptation. For the everyday person, applying these principles does not require elite facilities or genetic testing—it requires paying attention. Notice how you move, how you recover, when you feel strong, and when you feel drained. Adjust training accordingly, and over time, your body responds in kind.

Ultimately, decoding your genetic athletic profile is not about boxing yourself into categories but about expanding your awareness. You are not defined solely by your fiber type, nor confined to the limits of your DNA. You are the sum of your genes, the choices that shape their expression, and the rhythms that guide your daily performance. When these dimensions are understood and integrated, fitness ceases to be guesswork and becomes a precise dialogue between you and your body—a dialogue where you listen as much as you demand, and where adaptation is not forced but cultivated.

This is the essence of the adaptive body: a system capable of extraordinary transformation, provided we learn to read its language. By decoding the genetic and epigenetic signals, aligning with circadian rhythms, and applying training with precision, we step beyond generic prescriptions and into a personalized path toward potential. Fine fitness begins here, with the recognition that your body already contains the blueprint for greatness—it simply requires the right environment to bring it fully to life.

1.2 The Neuroplasticity Advantage in Physical Training

The human brain, once thought to be rigid and fixed in its wiring, is now understood to be one of the most adaptable organs in existence. Neuroplasticity—the capacity of the brain to reorganize itself by forming new neural connections—has transformed how we think about skill acquisition, learning, and even rehabilitation. In the context of fitness, neuroplasticity is the hidden advantage that allows training to extend beyond muscle and into the very architecture of the nervous system. Every repetition, every new movement pattern, and every challenge imposed on balance or coordination writes new instructions into the motor cortex, refining how the body executes physical tasks.

When you learn a new exercise, say a kettlebell swing or a complex yoga transition, the first barrier is rarely the strength of your muscles. It is the ability of your nervous system to coordinate firing patterns, recruit the right fibers in the right order, and inhibit competing signals. In the early stages of training, progress often appears rapid, not because muscle has suddenly grown, but because the brain has reorganized itself to execute the task more efficiently. This is neuroplasticity at work: a dynamic rewriting of the body's instruction manual so that movements become smoother, faster, and more precise.

Varied movement patterns accelerate this process. Repeating the same exercise endlessly does build efficiency, but introducing novel challenges expands the brain's repertoire. When the nervous system encounters unfamiliar stimuli—whether balancing on an unstable surface, attempting a new agility drill, or practicing with eyes closed—it is forced to create new pathways. These challenges engage deeper layers of proprioception, the sense of where the body exists in space. For example, balancing on a wobble board recruits not only the large postural muscles but also fine stabilizers that are often dormant on solid ground. Performing movements blindfolded further heightens proprioceptive intelligence by forcing the body to rely on internal feedback rather than visual cues. Over time, these experiences carve new neural grooves that make the body more resilient, responsive, and capable across a wide range of environments.

Another dimension of neuroplastic training is the use of visualization and micro-practice. The brain does not fully distinguish between a vividly imagined action and a physically executed one. Studies on athletes have shown that mental rehearsal activates many of the same neural circuits as actual movement. When a pianist imagines playing a piece, or when a sprinter visualizes exploding off the blocks, the motor cortex fires in patterns strikingly similar to physical practice. This capacity allows the creation of neural "superhighways" for complex movements even without constant physical repetition. By rehearsing mentally in detail—imagining the grip on a bar, the alignment of joints, the tempo of a stride—the brain refines pathways that later translate into smoother execution during real performance.

Micro-practice builds on this principle by breaking down movements into their smallest components and rehearsing them in short, concentrated bursts. Instead of exhausting the body with endless sets, micro-practice allows the nervous system to learn precision without fatigue clouding the signal. A dancer may repeat a single turn dozens of times, or a martial artist may practice the initial step of a kick repeatedly, each time strengthening the neural imprint. Over time, these fragments knit together into seamless patterns, supported by the brain's plasticity.

The practical implication is profound: training is not merely physical but neurological. Strength alone does not guarantee mastery; coordination and neural efficiency often determine success. By deliberately engaging the brain through varied patterns, proprioceptive challenges, visualization, and micro-practice, individuals can accelerate learning, reduce injury risk, and expand their capacity to adapt to new physical demands. Neuroplasticity is the reminder that the body and brain are inseparable in the journey toward fine fitness.

1.3 Biomarkers That Predict Peak Performance

While neuroplasticity helps explain how training sculpts both brain and body, another dimension of modern fitness lies in the measurement of internal signals—biomarkers that reveal how well the body is adapting. The pursuit of peak performance is not a guessing game. The body constantly communicates its state of readiness, stress, and recovery through measurable indicators, and learning to interpret them provides a roadmap for training smarter rather than harder.

One of the most powerful of these indicators is heart rate variability, or HRV. Unlike resting heart rate, which measures beats per minute, HRV tracks the subtle variations in time between each heartbeat. These fluctuations are controlled by the balance between the sympathetic and parasympathetic branches of the autonomic nervous system. A high HRV typically indicates strong parasympathetic activity, meaning the body is relaxed, recovered, and ready for exertion. A low HRV, on the other hand, can signal accumulated stress, fatigue, or insufficient recovery. Athletes who monitor HRV daily learn to adjust their training loads accordingly, pushing harder on days of high readiness and easing back when the nervous system signals strain. In this way, HRV becomes not just a number but a compass for aligning effort with the body's real capacity.

Cortisol, the body's primary stress hormone, offers another window into performance readiness. While acute spikes of cortisol during exercise are normal and even beneficial, chronically elevated levels can erode muscle tissue, suppress immune function, and impair recovery. Saliva testing provides a non-invasive way to measure cortisol fluctuations throughout the day, revealing whether the body is maintaining a healthy rhythm. Ideally, cortisol should peak in the morning to promote alertness and gradually decline toward evening, preparing the body for rest. When this pattern is disrupted—such as cortisol remaining high at night or failing to rise in the morning—it signals overtraining or chronic stress. Recognizing these shifts early allows interventions like adjusting intensity, incorporating recovery modalities, or prioritizing sleep before performance declines become visible.

Inflammation markers, too, hold critical insights. The body's inflammatory response is essential for healing microtears in muscle fibers and adapting to training stress. Yet when inflammation becomes excessive or chronic, it undermines both health and performance. C-reactive protein (CRP) and interleukin-6 (IL-6) are two biomarkers commonly measured in blood tests to assess this balance. Elevated CRP may indicate the body is struggling with systemic inflammation, often linked to inadequate recovery, poor nutrition, or hidden stressors such as lack of sleep. IL-6, while more complex in its signaling, can similarly reflect how the immune system is responding to training loads. Monitoring these markers provides athletes and everyday practitioners alike with actionable feedback: if levels remain consistently high, it may be time to increase recovery days, optimize nutrition with anti-inflammatory foods, or reduce external stress.

The integration of these biomarkers into training represents a shift from intuition alone to evidence-based precision. It is no longer enough to rely on subjective feelings of fatigue or energy; the body's internal data provides a more reliable guide. This does not mean reducing fitness to numbers alone, but rather using them as signposts in a larger journey. A runner who notices consistently low HRV may prevent injury by adjusting mileage before pain emerges. A lifter who identifies rising cortisol can scale back intensity before hitting a plateau. A coach monitoring CRP across a team can modify schedules to keep athletes primed for competition.

For those outside the professional athletic sphere, the value remains equally profound. Many individuals push through fatigue believing it to be normal, when in reality their biomarkers would reveal a body on the edge of breakdown. By learning to interpret these signals, fitness becomes more sustainable, resilient, and attuned to long-term well-being. Biomarkers are not abstract medical data but living indicators of how training, nutrition, sleep, and stress interact. They are the body's way of speaking clearly, provided we know how to listen.

Together, neuroplasticity and biomarkers illustrate two sides of the adaptive body. One shows how the brain rewires itself to expand potential, while the other reveals how the body communicates its readiness and limitations. Mastery of fitness lies in harnessing both: engaging the nervous system to accelerate learning and using biological signals to guide effort with precision. When combined, they form a partnership between awareness and measurement, intuition and science, practice and feedback.

This partnership is at the heart of fine fitness. It ensures that the journey toward strength, endurance, and mastery is not haphazard but intentional, informed by the body's capacity to adapt and its signals of when to push and when to pause. To ignore neuroplasticity is to neglect the brain's role in shaping movement. To ignore biomarkers is to gamble blindly with recovery and performance. But when both are embraced, training transcends guesswork and becomes a deliberate conversation with the adaptive body—one that continually evolves, learns, and refines itself on the path to peak human potential.

Chapter 2: Metabolic Flexibility — Engineering Your Energy Systems

"Elite athletes can switch between burning fat and carbohydrates 3x faster than sedentary individuals, burning up to 2,000 calories per hour at peak performance."

2.1 Training the Three Energy Systems Simultaneously

Every human movement, from lifting a coffee cup to running a marathon, is powered by the body's energy systems. These systems—phosphocreatine, glycolytic, and aerobic—operate not as isolated compartments but as overlapping gears in a single engine. At any given moment, all three contribute to fueling activity, with the balance shifting depending on intensity and duration. The mastery of metabolic flexibility lies in the ability to train these systems simultaneously, creating a body that can rapidly shift gears, sustain effort across diverse conditions, and recover efficiently between bursts of work.

The phosphocreatine system is the body's first responder. It powers the explosive, high-intensity efforts that last only seconds—like a sprint off the starting line, a heavy clean and jerk, or a vertical leap. This system relies on stored creatine phosphate in the muscles to rapidly regenerate ATP, the fundamental currency of cellular energy. But its reserves are limited, depleting in less than ten seconds of maximal effort. Training this system involves pushing the body into that short window of intensity, then allowing enough recovery for full replenishment before repeating. Six-second maximal efforts followed by three minutes of rest create the perfect environment for reinforcing this explosive capacity. The brief effort demands everything the phosphocreatine system can deliver, while the generous rest ensures the system is refueled, avoiding overlap with the glycolytic pathway. Over time, this practice strengthens not only raw power but also the efficiency of ATP regeneration, extending the ceiling of what can be achieved in short bursts.

The glycolytic system picks up where the phosphocreatine stores taper off, dominating in efforts lasting from about fifteen seconds to two minutes. It breaks down glucose to generate ATP quickly, producing lactate as a byproduct. For decades, lactate was misunderstood as a waste product responsible for fatigue, but research has reframed it as a shuttle molecule—a fuel that can be transported to other muscles or even the heart for energy. Training the glycolytic system, then, is about building tolerance to lactate and improving the body's ability to clear and recycle it. Protocols such as tempo intervals, where intensity is sustained just below the threshold of collapse, push the body to manage lactate effectively. For instance, alternating two-minute bursts of controlled effort with equal recovery teaches the muscles to buffer acidity and enhances enzymatic pathways that process glucose efficiently. Lactate shuttling protocols go further by designing workouts that intentionally flood the muscles with lactate, then require active recovery to redistribute and reuse it. This not only increases glycolytic capacity but also strengthens the bridge between anaerobic and aerobic metabolism.

While the phosphocreatine and glycolytic systems dominate short and middle ranges, the aerobic system is the backbone of human endurance. It uses oxygen to oxidize carbohydrates and fats, producing ATP in vast quantities compared to the other systems, though at a slower rate. The aerobic system powers hours of activity, from distance running to cycling, and even supports recovery between bouts of explosive effort. Training it efficiently requires a delicate balance. The polarized training model, used by many endurance champions, emphasizes spending roughly eighty percent of training time at low intensity and twenty percent at high intensity. The low-intensity sessions build a vast aerobic base, increasing mitochondrial density, capillary networks, and fat oxidation. The high-intensity sessions, on the other hand, stretch the upper limits of oxygen delivery and utilization, forcing adaptations that expand maximal capacity. Together, they create a system that can sustain effort for long periods yet still respond explosively when called upon.

What makes the human body remarkable is not simply the existence of these three systems but their seamless interaction. During a 400-meter sprint, for example, the phosphocreatine system fires off the starting line, the glycolytic system takes over as the pace continues, and the aerobic system contributes to recovery even as the runner collapses at the finish. During a soccer match, players cycle between short sprints, moderate jogs, and long stretches of positioning, constantly shifting between systems. In daily life, the same interplay occurs: rushing up stairs taps into phosphocreatine, carrying groceries across a parking lot leans on glycolytic pathways, and walking for an hour relies primarily on aerobic metabolism. Training the systems in isolation may build narrow capacity, but training them simultaneously develops metabolic flexibility—the ability to adapt energy delivery to any demand.

Designing workouts that integrate these systems is both art and science. A session might begin with short, all-out sprints to ignite the phosphocreatine pathway, followed by intervals at controlled intensity to stress glycolytic tolerance, and finish with sustained low-intensity work to expand aerobic endurance. In this way, the body is exposed to the full spectrum of demands in a single session, learning not only to perform within each system but also to transition smoothly between them. Recovery becomes faster, fatigue management improves, and performance in diverse contexts—from weightlifting competitions to long hikes—rises dramatically.

Another key element in training all three systems is understanding how they fuel one another. The aerobic system, though slower, plays a crucial role in replenishing phosphocreatine stores between sprints. Likewise, lactate produced in glycolysis is recycled through aerobic pathways. By strengthening the aerobic base, an athlete indirectly improves their capacity for repeated explosive efforts, as recovery time shortens. Conversely, training the phosphocreatine and glycolytic systems builds the ability to push beyond thresholds where the aerobic system alone cannot keep pace. This synergy ensures that no matter the situation, the body has a versatile engine ready to switch gears instantly.

It is also important to recognize that metabolic flexibility is not reserved for elite athletes. Everyday life demands constant shifts in energy systems, whether it is chasing after children, climbing multiple flights of stairs, or cycling to work. A sedentary body, unused to these transitions, tires easily and recovers slowly, while a trained body moves seamlessly from one system to the next. In this sense, training the three systems simultaneously is not only about sport but also about equipping the body for resilience in daily living. The ability to sprint when needed, sustain activity for long hours, and recover without collapse is the essence of functional fitness.

The challenge for most people is balancing the demands of all three systems without overtraining. Because the phosphocreatine and glycolytic systems rely heavily on high intensity, they place significant stress on the nervous system and musculature. Too much emphasis on these pathways without adequate recovery can lead to burnout. Conversely, overemphasizing the aerobic system without intensity can lead to stagnation. This is where intelligent programming comes into play: alternating sessions, monitoring recovery, and listening to the body's signals. The ultimate goal is not perfection in any one system but harmony across all three, where none lags so far behind that it becomes a limiting factor.

At its core, training the energy systems simultaneously teaches the body adaptability. The phosphocreatine pathway provides the explosive spark, the glycolytic system offers the bridge of intensity, and the aerobic foundation ensures durability. Together, they create an engine capable of extraordinary output, one that does not break down under stress but instead shifts gears smoothly, conserving and deploying energy with precision. Metabolic flexibility is not simply about burning fat or carbohydrates more efficiently; it is about orchestrating these three systems into a symphony of performance that can meet the unpredictable demands of both sport and life.

When these systems are deliberately trained, the body learns to handle extremes without fear. The six-second sprint prepares you for the sudden demand of urgency. The lactate-filled interval builds resilience against discomfort and sharpens recovery. The long, easy run or ride strengthens the foundation that sustains it all. Together, they weave resilience into every layer of physiology, ensuring that energy is never a barrier but a resource to be deployed with confidence.

2.2 Nutritional Periodization for Energy System Development

The training of energy systems is not accomplished through exercise alone. Nutrition, timed and structured with precision, is equally critical in shaping how the body produces, stores, and utilizes energy. Nutritional periodization—the deliberate adjustment of macronutrient intake across days, weeks, or training cycles—provides the metabolic stimulus that guides adaptation at the cellular level. Just as an athlete alternates between strength days and endurance days, the body can be taught to burn fuel more efficiently by alternating between phases of carbohydrate emphasis, fat reliance, and carefully timed nutrient loading.

Strategic carbohydrate cycling is one of the most effective tools for enhancing mitochondrial biogenesis, the process by which new mitochondria are created within cells. Mitochondria are the engines of aerobic metabolism, and the more abundant and efficient they become, the greater the body's capacity to sustain activity through oxygen-driven pathways. Carbohydrate restriction at key times forces the body to rely more heavily on fat and stimulates molecular signals, such as PGC-1α, that promote mitochondrial growth. Yet this does not mean carbohydrates are abandoned entirely. Rather, they are periodized: consumed in higher amounts before demanding training sessions where glycolytic power is needed, and reduced on lighter days or recovery phases to encourage fat adaptation. The alternation between high and low carbohydrate availability teaches the body to be metabolically flexible, able to switch between fuels with agility.

Targeted ketogenic phases further refine this adaptation. A strict ketogenic state, where carbohydrate intake is minimized to the point of producing ketone bodies as alternative fuel, trains the body to oxidize fat at rates 25 to 50 percent higher than in carbohydrate-dominant states. While not necessary year-round, short cycles of ketogenic nutrition—lasting anywhere from a week to several weeks—provide a reset that heightens fat metabolism. For endurance athletes, this means the ability to rely more heavily on the nearly limitless fat stores in the body, sparing glycogen for high-intensity surges. For strength athletes, it may improve recovery efficiency by reducing reliance on constant glycogen replenishment. The key lies not in permanence but in cycling: using ketogenic phases as strategic tools rather than lifestyle absolutes.

The precision of nutrient timing adds another layer of control. Glycogen supercompensation—the rapid storage of carbohydrates in muscle after depletion—is maximized when nutrients are consumed within a narrow 15-minute window after exhaustive exercise. During this window, muscles are uniquely primed to absorb glucose and rebuild glycogen stores at rates up to double the normal capacity. Athletes who refuel immediately after training not only restore energy faster but also increase the total glycogen ceiling, providing a larger reserve for future efforts. In practical terms, this means finishing an intense interval session and consuming a targeted blend of carbohydrate and protein without delay, rather than waiting an hour. Over time, the discipline of timing magnifies the efficiency of training by ensuring that every depletion phase is followed by maximal restoration.

Nutritional periodization is as much about restraint as it is about fueling. By deliberately alternating between phases of restriction and abundance, the body learns resilience. Just as constant intensity in training leads to stagnation, constant abundance in nutrition dulls adaptation. The cycles of scarcity and replenishment are what teach the metabolic machinery to adapt, expand, and strengthen. It is in this balance—feeding when performance demands it, withholding when adaptation requires it—that the energy systems are sculpted into versatility.

2.3 The Breath-Metabolism Connection

If nutrition provides the raw materials for energy, breathing governs how efficiently those materials are converted into usable fuel. Often treated as an unconscious reflex, breathing is in fact a powerful lever for metabolic control. By altering the rhythm, depth, and composition of breath, it is possible to shift how the body delivers oxygen, manages carbon dioxide, and regulates acid-base balance during exertion. Breath training has long been used by freedivers and yogis to push the limits of human tolerance, but in recent years athletes and scientists alike have recognized its direct role in energy system development.

Controlled hypoxic breathing is one method that reshapes the metabolic landscape. By intentionally reducing oxygen availability during specific training bouts, the body is stimulated to produce more erythropoietin (EPO), the hormone that drives red blood cell production. More red blood cells mean more oxygen-carrying capacity, a natural enhancement that mirrors the adaptations of altitude training without the need to relocate to high mountains. Short intervals of breath-holding after exhalation or training with restricted airflow can trigger this adaptive pathway, provided they are used sparingly and with respect for the body's limits. The outcome is an enhanced ability to deliver oxygen to working muscles, extending endurance and delaying fatigue in high-demand efforts.

Equally important is the training of carbon dioxide tolerance. Most people think the urge to breathe is caused by a lack of oxygen, but in reality, it is the accumulation of carbon dioxide that drives respiratory discomfort. By practicing controlled exposure to elevated CO2 levels—through extended breath holds or slow, deep breathing during exertion—the body learns to tolerate higher concentrations without panic. This adaptation delays the point at which lactate accumulation forces a drop in performance. By improving CO2 tolerance, athletes can sustain efforts 20 to 30 percent longer before acidosis impairs muscle function. It is a subtle yet profound shift: the body becomes comfortable operating in conditions that would previously have signaled emergency, unlocking reserves of endurance and composure.

Metabolic breathing patterns provide another dimension of real-time control. The respiratory exchange ratio (RER), which measures the balance between carbon dioxide produced and oxygen consumed, reveals whether the body is burning primarily fats or carbohydrates at a given moment. Through conscious breathing techniques, RER can be nudged in one direction or another. Deep, slow breathing favors fat oxidation, as it supports steady oxygen delivery and stabilizes blood gases. Rapid, shallow breathing shifts metabolism toward carbohydrate use, preparing for explosive bursts. Athletes who master these patterns can, quite literally, control their fuel selection with their breath, matching the demands of activity with the optimal substrate. For example, a marathoner may use slow diaphragmatic breathing early in a race to maximize fat use, then switch to more rapid breathing in the final sprint to tap into glycogen reserves.

The integration of breathing into metabolic training also has profound psychological effects. Controlled breath regulates the nervous system, calming the sympathetic drive and enhancing focus. In moments of high exertion, when the mind threatens to spiral into panic, breath provides a tether to stability. This mental composure feeds back into physiology, as reduced anxiety prevents unnecessary spikes in heart rate and cortisol. Breath, therefore, is not just a mechanical function but a mediator between mind and metabolism.

The marriage of nutritional periodization and breath control epitomizes the holistic approach to metabolic flexibility. One provides the substrate and timing, the other dictates the efficiency and selection of that substrate in real time. Together, they form a system where the body is not only fueled intelligently but also guided with precision through the act of breathing. This integration transforms training from brute force into strategy, where every inhalation and every meal contribute to a finely tuned engine capable of extraordinary adaptability.

Metabolic flexibility, then, is not a mystery reserved for elites. It is the natural inheritance of every human body, waiting to be cultivated. Through cycling nutrition to guide cellular adaptation and mastering breath to command metabolic balance, anyone can teach their physiology to switch gears effortlessly. The result is a body that no longer fears the depletion of one fuel source or the onset of fatigue, but one that thrives in the dynamic dance of oxygen, carbon dioxide, fats, and carbohydrates. The convergence of these practices ensures that energy, the foundation of all movement, is never the limiting factor but the gateway to performance, resilience, and flow.

Chapter 3: The Architecture of Movement — Building Functional Strength Through Pattern Mastery

"Research shows that mastering just seven fundamental movement patterns can reduce injury risk by 73% while improving athletic performance across all sports."

3.1 Spiral Dynamics and Rotational Power

The human body is not designed to move in straight lines alone. Every step, every throw, and every strike of force carries within it spirals, rotations, and counter-rotations that transfer energy with elegance and efficiency. This is the essence of spiral dynamics, a principle rooted in the body's fascial architecture and neurological control. When we examine movement through this lens, it becomes clear that true functional strength is not just about pushing forward or pulling back, but about harnessing rotation—developing the ability to coil, release, and stabilize energy through spiraling pathways that run from the ground to the fingertips.

The connective tissue network, known as fascia, provides the structural foundation for this dynamic. Fascia is not inert wrapping around muscles but a living, tensile web that transmits force across the body. When trained appropriately, it behaves like an elastic spring, storing energy as it lengthens and releasing it explosively when recoiled. Consider the simple act of throwing a ball. The motion begins with a rotation of the hips and trunk, stretching the fascial lines that run diagonally across the torso. As the arm whips forward, that stored energy is unleashed, amplifying power far beyond what isolated muscle contraction could provide. This is elastic recoil in action, and it is central to both athletic performance and daily movement efficiency.

Training elastic recoil requires movements that load and unload these fascial lines in rhythmic cycles. Oscillatory patterns—such as repeated side-to-side medicine ball throws against a wall or whip-like band drills—teach the tissue to lengthen under tension and rebound with speed. Unlike traditional strength training that emphasizes slow, linear contractions, these drills prioritize elasticity and rhythm. Over time, the body learns not only to generate more force but also to conserve energy by using stored elastic potential instead of relying solely on muscular effort. The result is movement that feels lighter, faster, and more resilient.

Rotational power depends on more than fascial recoil. It also arises from the coordinated creation of force couples, where opposing muscles and segments of the body work together to generate torque. Imagine a golfer at the top of a swing: the hips begin to rotate forward while the shoulders remain momentarily back, creating a stretch across the torso. This separation, often called the "X-factor" in sports science, is what produces extraordinary rotational force when the shoulders finally follow through. Training this separation can be done with tools like cable machines, which allow controlled resistance through twisting patterns, or with medicine balls, which provide dynamic load in rotational throws. By practicing these patterns under varying resistance, athletes and everyday movers alike condition their nervous systems to coordinate hips, trunk, and shoulders into efficient rotational chains.

Cable systems offer unique advantages because they permit rotation under constant tension and across different planes of motion. A standing cable chop, for example, challenges the body to coordinate a diagonal pull from high to low, engaging the obliques, lats, and hips in a seamless pattern. Medicine ball variations, on the other hand, emphasize explosive release. A rotational slam or side throw demands not just strength but timing and speed, teaching the body to unleash energy at the exact moment when torque is maximized. Both approaches complement one another: cables for control and integration, medicine balls for speed and power.

But with rotation comes the necessity of control. Just as the body must know how to create torque, it must also know how to resist it. Anti-rotation stability is what protects the spine and pelvis from collapsing under rotational forces. Without it, the transfer of energy leaks, leading to inefficiency at best and injury at worst. The Pallof press, a deceptively simple exercise where the body resists being pulled into rotation by an anchored cable or band, is a cornerstone for developing this stability. By holding the spine steady against lateral force, the deep core musculature is taught to brace and stabilize, creating a protective sheath around the lumbar region. Progressions—from static holds to dynamic presses or step-outs—expand this capacity, preparing the body for the unpredictable rotations of sport and life.

Unilateral loading provides another layer of anti-rotation training. Carrying a heavy weight on one side of the body, as in a suitcase carry or single-arm overhead walk, forces the torso to resist lateral collapse. The asymmetry stimulates not only the obliques and spinal stabilizers but also the hips and shoulders, ensuring that every link in the chain contributes to maintaining alignment. This type of training develops a quiet strength, less visible than explosive throws but equally essential. It teaches the body to remain solid under pressure, a prerequisite for safely generating and absorbing rotational power.

The integration of elastic recoil, force couples, and anti-rotation stability paints a complete picture of spiral dynamics. Each element alone offers benefits, but together they transform the body into a system capable of moving fluidly and powerfully across multiple planes. This integration is not theoretical—it shows up in every athletic domain. A boxer's punch is not a simple arm strike but a whip of rotational force beginning from the feet. A tennis serve is not just a shoulder action but a spiraling sequence of hips, trunk, and arm. Even the simple act of walking involves alternating spirals through the torso that balance and propel the body forward.

What is often overlooked is that rotational training is not solely for athletes. In daily life, lifting a suitcase into a car, shoveling soil in a garden, or twisting to reach a shelf all demand spiral coordination. When the body is not trained for these movements, strain accumulates in the spine or shoulders, leading to chronic discomfort. By mastering spiral dynamics, individuals not only improve athletic performance but also safeguard themselves against the mundane injuries of daily living. Functional strength is not measured solely by what can be lifted in the gym but by how well the body carries out the rotations and counter-rotations embedded in real life.

Spiral training also reshapes the nervous system's understanding of movement. When the brain perceives that the body can rotate powerfully and stabilize effectively, it unlocks greater freedom of motion. Fear and hesitation often limit performance more than physical capacity. A body confident in its spiraling strength is one that moves with fluid assurance, whether in the heat of competition or the rhythm of daily activity. This confidence translates into efficiency, as the nervous system stops bracing unnecessarily and allows energy to flow through the rotational chains.

Ultimately, spiral dynamics and rotational power embody the principle that movement is architecture. Just as a well-designed building channels weight through arches and spirals for strength and resilience, the human body channels force through its fascial lines and rotational sequences. By training these structures deliberately, we construct a body that is both powerful and durable, capable of generating torque without breaking down, capable of absorbing force without faltering. It is the architecture of functional strength, one built not only on raw muscle but on the intelligent integration of rotation, recoil, and stability.

The mastery of spiral dynamics marks a turning point in fitness. It shifts the focus from linear, isolated training to multi-dimensional, integrated movement. It acknowledges that the body is not a collection of parts but a unified system where every twist, brace, and release contributes to the whole. And most importantly, it reconnects training to the patterns of life itself, where nothing moves in straight lines and every action unfolds in spirals.

3.2 Velocity-Based Training for Power Development

Power lies at the intersection of force and speed. Strength without speed produces sluggish motion, while speed without force results in fragility. To cultivate power—the ability to generate maximum force in minimum time—athletes and practitioners alike must learn to manipulate both variables deliberately. Velocity-based training, often abbreviated as VBT, has emerged as one of the most precise methods for bridging this gap. By monitoring bar speed, adjusting resistance dynamically, and incorporating ballistic strategies, VBT transforms the training environment from guesswork into measurable progress.

At its core, velocity-based training is about aligning movement with the force-velocity curve, which illustrates the inverse relationship between load and speed. Heavy loads move slowly but produce maximal force, while lighter loads move quickly but with reduced force output. Training across this spectrum ensures that the nervous system is prepared to generate power in multiple contexts. Bar speed monitoring, using modern devices or even smartphone applications, allows lifters to target precise velocity zones. For example, performing squats or presses at bar speeds between 0.5 and 1.3 meters per second develops strength-speed qualities ideal for explosive athletics. This transforms lifting from a subjective experience into quantifiable data. Instead of simply loading a bar with arbitrary weight, the athlete adjusts resistance to maintain velocity within the desired range, ensuring every repetition is targeted and efficient.

Accommodating resistance takes this principle further by altering the resistance profile of an exercise to match the body's natural strength curve. Traditional weights provide constant load, which can under-stimulate muscles in strong positions and overburden them in weaker ones. By adding bands or chains to a barbell, resistance increases as leverage improves. Bands stretch and chains rise from the floor, both intensifying load at the top of a movement where the body is strongest. This trains athletes to accelerate through the entire range of motion rather than slowing down near the end. The result is a powerful emphasis on strength-speed development: the nervous system learns not to coast, but to push with maximum intent until the very last degree of extension.

Ballistic training introduces yet another layer of neurological recruitment. Unlike controlled lifts where deceleration is inevitable, ballistic movements demand acceleration throughout the entire range, often releasing the load into free space. Medicine ball throws, jump squats, and bench throws are classic examples. By eliminating the braking phase, ballistic training recruits Type II muscle fibers—the fast-twitch fibers responsible for explosive output—with unmatched efficiency. Coupled with compensatory acceleration, where even heavy loads are moved with the intent to accelerate as rapidly as possible, this approach reconditions the nervous system to fire with maximal intensity. It is not simply about moving weight, but about moving it with intent, speed, and aggression.

The beauty of velocity-based training lies in its adaptability. On days when fatigue dulls performance, bar speed provides immediate feedback, prompting adjustments in load to preserve quality. On days when the nervous system is primed, the same monitoring reveals opportunities to push harder. This dynamic responsiveness ensures that training is always aligned with the athlete's state, reducing the risk of overtraining while maximizing adaptation. Over time, this results not only in measurable increases in power but also in a body conditioned to accelerate under any circumstance.

3.3 Isometric Training for Neural Drive Enhancement

If velocity-based training sharpens the output of force and speed, isometric training strengthens the nervous system's command over muscle recruitment. Unlike dynamic movements, isometrics involve holding or resisting against an immovable load, producing no visible change in joint angle but profound changes in neural drive. By training the nervous system to fire more motor units at once, isometrics enhance strength, break through plateaus, and fortify tissues against injury.

Overcoming isometrics are particularly effective for addressing weak points within a lift. In this method, the athlete pushes or pulls against an immovable object—such as pressing a barbell into pins fixed in a rack—at specific joint angles. The nervous system responds by ramping motor unit recruitment to maximum levels, often far beyond what can be achieved in dynamic lifting. Because there is no movement, the stress is concentrated at the chosen angle, making this strategy ideal for targeting sticking points in exercises like squats or bench presses. With repeated practice, the neural adaptations carry over into full range movements, unlocking strength that was previously inaccessible.

Yielding isometrics, by contrast, focus on resisting external load for extended durations, training the muscles' eccentric and stabilizing capacities. Holding a heavy weight in mid-position until failure, or resisting against bands that pull the body into unwanted positions, develops resilience in the very structures most prone to injury. Tendons and ligaments, which adapt more slowly than muscle, particularly benefit from this time-under-tension stimulus. Yielding isometrics also cultivate mental toughness, teaching the body to endure strain without collapse, a skill as useful in daily life as it is in sport.

A particularly powerful application of isometric training comes when it is combined with plyometric movements in a technique known as post-activation potentiation. Here, an isometric hold at near-maximal intensity is immediately followed by an explosive action, such as a jump or throw. The nervous system, having been primed by the isometric contraction, fires with heightened vigor during the subsequent plyometric, resulting in power increases of fifteen to thirty percent. This method takes advantage of the nervous system's readiness, temporarily unlocking levels of force production otherwise dormant. For athletes, this means sharper sprints, higher jumps, and faster strikes; for the everyday mover, it means discovering reserves of explosiveness that improve balance, agility, and responsiveness.

The neural benefits of isometric training extend beyond strength and power. Because isometrics demand full concentration, they deepen the mind-body connection, teaching the practitioner to feel the subtleties of muscular engagement. Holding a position under load forces awareness of posture, alignment, and breathing. This awareness, cultivated over time, spills into all movement, refining technique and reducing wasted effort. By learning to activate muscles deliberately in stillness, the body becomes more coordinated in motion.

Isometric training also carries the advantage of accessibility. It requires minimal equipment, can be practiced in small spaces, and places less strain on joints than high-load dynamic lifting. For individuals rehabilitating from injury or seeking to build foundational strength, it provides a safe yet potent avenue for progress. At the same time, for advanced athletes, its ability to stimulate neural drive makes it an indispensable complement to explosive training.

Taken together, velocity-based training and isometric methods represent two ends of a spectrum. One emphasizes movement at maximum speed, the other emphasizes force without movement. Yet both converge on the same goal: enhancing the nervous system's capacity to recruit muscle fibers efficiently, powerfully, and safely. When integrated into a larger program, they create a body that is not only strong in the traditional sense but also neurologically sharp, adaptable, and resilient.

The architecture of movement is incomplete without these dimensions. Spiral dynamics and rotational power teach the body to move through space with elegance, but velocity and isometric training teach the body how to command its own force at the extremes of motion. Power is sculpted in the intent to accelerate, and stability is forged in the capacity to resist. Together, they weave a fabric of strength that is both dynamic and enduring, capable of responding to the unpredictable demands of sport and life alike.

Chapter 4: The Nutrition Matrix — Precision Fueling for Performance

"The timing of a single meal can alter gene expression for up to 48 hours, affecting everything from muscle protein synthesis to cognitive function."

4.1 Chrono-Nutrition and Meal Timing Optimization

Nutrition is often discussed in terms of quantity and quality, but timing is an equally powerful variable, one that can reshape how the body processes, stores, and utilizes fuel. Chrono-nutrition, the science of aligning food intake with the body's circadian rhythms, has emerged as a critical frontier in performance and health. The human body is not a static machine but a dynamic system governed by biological clocks. These clocks influence everything from hormone secretion to enzymatic activity, meaning that the same meal can have profoundly different effects depending on when it is consumed. Understanding and harnessing these rhythms allows us to unlock the full potential of nutrition, turning meals from mere sustenance into precise instruments of adaptation.

One of the most compelling applications of chrono-nutrition lies in the synchronization of protein intake with the body's natural peaks of muscle protein synthesis. Muscles are in a constant state of turnover, breaking down and rebuilding fibers in response to activity and stress. After exercise, this rebuilding accelerates, but the effect is transient, peaking and then declining if nutrients are not supplied. Research has shown that consuming protein every three to four hours maintains an elevated state of muscle protein synthesis, effectively extending the window in which muscles rebuild and strengthen. This rhythm ensures that the raw materials for recovery are consistently available, transforming scattered protein consumption into a steady cadence that maximizes adaptation. For athletes, this might mean structuring meals and snacks around evenly spaced intervals, each containing a high-quality protein source. For the everyday individual, it could simply mean paying attention to the distribution of protein across the day rather than clustering it into one large serving at dinner.

While protein distribution supports muscle growth and repair, the concept of time-restricted feeding speaks to a broader cellular rhythm. Limiting food intake to defined windows—commonly eight to ten hours within the day—has been shown to enhance autophagy, the process by which cells recycle damaged components and renew themselves. Autophagy is not constant; it thrives during fasting states when nutrient availability is low. By aligning eating patterns with this rhythm, individuals can create daily cycles of nourishment and renewal, feeding cells when they are primed to build and cleansing them when they are primed to repair. The benefits extend beyond performance into longevity, as cellular renewal plays a central role in delaying aging processes and reducing the risk of chronic disease. Importantly, time-restricted feeding is not about eating less but about eating within windows that amplify the body's innate cycles.

The power of meal timing becomes particularly evident when considering the overnight period. Sleep is when some of the most significant hormonal events occur, including the release of growth hormone, which drives tissue repair and metabolic regulation. Pre-sleep nutrition, when designed with precision, can amplify these nocturnal processes. A slow-digesting protein, such as casein, consumed before bed, provides a steady stream of amino acids throughout the night, ensuring that muscles remain in a positive balance rather than drifting into catabolism. Carbohydrates consumed in the evening can also play a role, not only replenishing glycogen but improving serotonin availability, which supports deeper sleep. Far from disrupting rest, strategic pre-sleep nutrition can enhance recovery, aligning with the body's nocturnal repair cycle to produce more profound adaptation by morning.

Chrono-nutrition also influences cognitive function. The brain, like the muscles, responds differently to nutrients depending on timing. A carbohydrate-rich breakfast may improve alertness by raising serotonin levels and supporting neurotransmitter synthesis, while a protein-focused morning meal may sharpen concentration by providing precursors for dopamine. Later in the day, lighter meals that avoid large spikes in glucose may prevent the afternoon crash in energy and focus. By aligning meals with the ebb and flow of cognitive rhythms, nutrition becomes a tool not only for physical performance but also for mental clarity.

An often-overlooked element of meal timing is its impact on gene expression. Nutrients act as signals to the body's clock genes, which regulate the rhythm of cellular activity. A meal rich in certain macronutrients at one time of day may activate pathways of energy storage, while the same meal consumed at a different time may activate pathways of energy expenditure. For example, insulin sensitivity is generally higher in the morning, meaning that carbohydrates are more likely to be used for immediate energy rather than stored as fat. By contrast, consuming the same carbohydrates late at night, when insulin sensitivity is lower, may promote storage rather than oxidation. Aligning intake with these natural fluctuations ensures that food supports performance rather than working against it.

This temporal dimension of nutrition also connects with training itself. Pre-exercise meals provide fuel for performance, but post-exercise meals determine how well recovery unfolds. A carefully timed combination of carbohydrates and protein immediately after training amplifies glycogen storage and muscle protein synthesis, capitalizing on the heightened sensitivity of tissues in that window. Delaying intake by even an hour can blunt these effects, reducing the efficiency of recovery. Thus, meal timing is not simply about the clock but about aligning intake with the physiological state of the body—whether it is primed for exertion, recovery, or rest.

For those pursuing metabolic flexibility, chrono-nutrition offers yet another lever. Training in a fasted state, typically in the morning before the first meal, encourages the body to rely more heavily on fat oxidation. Eating after such sessions then provides the fuel for recovery and adaptation. On other days, consuming carbohydrates before high-intensity sessions ensures maximal glycolytic output. By alternating these strategies within the framework of circadian timing, individuals can sculpt their energy systems to perform across a spectrum of demands.

The discipline of chrono-nutrition is not about rigid rules but about awareness. It is the recognition that the body does not respond uniformly throughout the day, and that food can either harmonize with its rhythms or disrupt them. For the modern individual, whose schedules often push meals into late nights or scatter them haphazardly, this awareness can be transformative. By restoring alignment between when we eat and how our bodies are designed to process nutrients, we reclaim efficiency, resilience, and vitality.

Ultimately, chrono-nutrition and meal timing optimization represent a shift in perspective. Nutrition is no longer reduced to counting calories or grams of protein, but elevated to a dynamic dialogue with the body's rhythms. Every meal becomes an opportunity to reinforce cycles of performance, recovery, and renewal. Every fast becomes a space for cleansing and repair. Every pre-sleep snack becomes a bridge to deeper recovery. When viewed through this lens, food is not simply fuel but time-sensitive information, a message delivered to the body that shapes its adaptation for hours and even days to come.

4.2 Micronutrient Synergy and Absorption Enhancement

While macronutrients provide the bulk of energy and structural building blocks for the body, micronutrients act as the silent directors of countless physiological processes. Vitamins, minerals, and phytonutrients regulate enzyme activity, signal hormonal cascades, and determine how effectively macronutrients are used. For athletes and anyone seeking performance and recovery, the difference between sufficiency and optimization often lies not in consuming more calories but in ensuring that micronutrients are absorbed and utilized at their highest potential.

Micronutrients rarely act in isolation. They are part of a complex web where one enhances or limits the function of another. Vitamin D, for example, is central to calcium metabolism and bone health, but without vitamin K2, calcium may be deposited in arteries rather than bones. Magnesium, in turn, is required to activate vitamin D into its usable form. Taken together, vitamin D, K2, and magnesium form a nutrient stack that increases bioavailability and efficiency by two to three times compared to consuming each individually. This synergy illustrates the importance of seeing nutrition not as isolated inputs but as coordinated systems.

Athletic performance places unique demands on micronutrient stores, and deficiencies are more common than many realize. Iron, for instance, is critical for oxygen transport through hemoglobin, yet endurance athletes often struggle with depleted iron levels due to repetitive foot strikes, sweat losses, and increased turnover. Even mild iron deficiency can lead to fatigue, slower recovery, and diminished aerobic capacity. B12, another oxygen-related nutrient, is essential for red blood cell formation and neurological function. Plant-based athletes are particularly at risk of deficiency, as B12 is found almost exclusively in animal products. Zinc, required for immune function and protein synthesis, is rapidly depleted through sweat. Omega-3 fatty acids, though technically macronutrients, behave like regulatory molecules, reducing inflammation and supporting cardiovascular efficiency. When optimized, these nutrients create a performance environment where energy delivery is smooth, recovery is accelerated, and resilience to stress is heightened.

The challenge lies not only in consuming these nutrients but in ensuring their absorption. Iron, for example, is absorbed more effectively when paired with vitamin C but inhibited when consumed with calcium or tannins found in tea and coffee. Zinc absorption is influenced by phytates present in grains and legumes, but soaking or fermenting these foods reduces inhibition. Omega-3 fatty acids from fish or algae are more effective when consumed alongside fat-containing meals, which enhance bioavailability. Attention to such pairings transforms nutrition from a scattershot approach into a precise strategy.

Another layer of optimization comes from phytonutrient cycling. Phytonutrients, such as polyphenols and carotenoids, provide antioxidant protection and modulate cellular pathways. However, constant high doses of antioxidants can blunt training adaptations by reducing the mild oxidative stress that signals the body to grow stronger. The solution is not to abandon antioxidants but to cycle their intake. On high-intensity training days, moderate doses support recovery without dampening adaptation, while on rest days, larger amounts of colorful fruits and vegetables can be consumed to maximize cellular renewal. This rhythmic approach ensures that the protective benefits of antioxidants are achieved without disrupting the hormetic stress that drives progress.

Micronutrient synergy, therefore, is not about chasing superfoods or supplements in isolation. It is about orchestrating timing, combinations, and cycles to create an environment where every nutrient amplifies the effectiveness of the others. This orchestration acknowledges the body's complexity and leverages it to create performance gains that cannot be achieved through macronutrient management alone.

4.3 Gut Microbiome Optimization for Athletes

The digestive tract is far more than a passive tube for processing food. It is a living ecosystem, home to trillions of bacteria that outnumber human cells and collectively form the gut microbiome. These microorganisms influence nutrient absorption, immune function, inflammation, and even mood and cognition. For athletes, the state of the microbiome can determine whether nutrients are absorbed efficiently, whether the gut withstands the stress of exertion, and whether recovery unfolds smoothly. Optimizing the microbiome is therefore a cornerstone of precision fueling.

Performance-enhancing bacterial strains are not a fantasy of science fiction but a reality uncovered by recent research. Certain strains of bacteria, such as *Veillonella atypica*, thrive on lactate and convert it into propionate, a short-chain fatty acid that fuels endurance. Studies on marathon runners have shown that these strains proliferate after long races, suggesting a natural adaptation of the microbiome to athletic stress. By cultivating beneficial strains through targeted prebiotic and probiotic protocols, athletes can tilt their microbial balance toward performance support. Prebiotics, found in fibers from foods like garlic, onions, and bananas, feed beneficial bacteria, while probiotics—live microorganisms from sources such as yogurt, kefir, or specialized supplements—directly introduce supportive strains. Together, they create a gut environment tuned to absorb nutrients more effectively and produce metabolites that enhance endurance and recovery.

Fermented foods are particularly valuable in this process. Beyond introducing beneficial bacteria, they improve nutrient bioavailability. Fermentation breaks down compounds that inhibit absorption, such as phytates, while producing enzymes that aid digestion. For athletes who struggle with gastrointestinal distress during training, fermented foods can also reduce gut permeability—a common issue where intense exercise increases the passage of unwanted particles through the intestinal lining, leading to inflammation and discomfort. By strengthening the integrity of the gut barrier, fermented foods mitigate these risks and support smoother performance. Sauerkraut, kimchi, miso, and kombucha are not merely culinary curiosities but powerful allies in digestive resilience.

A structured approach to gut optimization is often framed as the 4R protocol: remove, replace, reinoculate, and repair. First, irritants that disrupt the microbiome—such as excessive processed foods, alcohol, or allergens—are removed. Then digestive aids, such as enzymes or bile acids if needed, are introduced to replace what is lacking. Next, beneficial bacteria are reinoculated through probiotics and prebiotics. Finally, the gut lining is repaired with nutrients like glutamine, zinc carnosine, and omega-3s. This cyclical process rebuilds the digestive system into a more efficient, resilient state. For athletes, it means not only fewer gut problems during training but also improved extraction of micronutrients, better regulation of inflammation, and enhanced recovery capacity.

The connection between the microbiome and systemic performance extends even to the brain. Gut bacteria produce neurotransmitters and influence the gut-brain axis, shaping mood, focus, and stress resilience. An optimized microbiome reduces anxiety responses to stress and supports mental clarity, both of which are critical for peak performance under pressure. This mind-gut link emphasizes that fueling is not just about calories or nutrients but about cultivating the ecosystem that manages their use.

When micronutrient synergy and microbiome optimization are combined, the Nutrition Matrix becomes fully alive. Micronutrients ensure that the cellular machinery operates with precision, while the microbiome ensures that these nutrients are delivered, absorbed, and regulated in ways that enhance performance. Together, they turn nutrition from a mechanical input into a dynamic dialogue between the body and its environment.

Chapter 5: Recovery Architecture — The Science of Supercompensation

"Professional athletes spend 3x more time on recovery than training, yet 90% of fitness enthusiasts ignore this performance multiplier entirely."

5.1 Sleep Engineering for Athletic Excellence

In the world of performance, training often steals the spotlight. Workouts are documented, measured, and glorified, while recovery tends to fade into the background as an afterthought. Yet recovery, and sleep in particular, is where the real transformation occurs. Muscles do not grow stronger during the last rep of a squat or the final sprint of a session—they grow stronger in the hours afterward, when the body enters states of repair and adaptation. The same is true for the nervous system, the immune system, and even cognition. Sleep is the architect of supercompensation, the biological process through which the body rebounds from stress to a level higher than before. Without it, training is little more than controlled damage. With it, training becomes a platform for transformation.

Sleep is not a monolithic state but a cycle composed of stages that repeat throughout the night. Light sleep, deep slow-wave sleep, and rapid eye movement (REM) sleep each serve distinct purposes. Slow-wave sleep restores the body physically, releasing growth hormone and repairing tissues. REM sleep restores the mind, consolidating skills and integrating memories, including motor patterns learned in training. The cycling between these stages is what creates complete recovery. For athletes and fitness enthusiasts, optimizing this architecture is not about chasing more hours of sleep alone, but about maximizing the quality of those hours by aligning them with environmental cues and deliberate strategies.

Temperature is one of the most potent levers for shaping sleep architecture. The body's core temperature naturally declines as it prepares for rest, signaling the onset of deep sleep. By aligning the sleep environment with this process, recovery can be deepened. A room cooled to between 65 and 68 degrees Fahrenheit supports this thermoregulatory shift, allowing the body to sink into slow-wave sleep more efficiently. Conversely, environments that are too warm disrupt the natural cooling process, leading to frequent awakenings and reduced time spent in restorative stages. Simple interventions, such as breathable bedding, cooling mattresses, or pre-sleep rituals like warm showers that trigger a rebound cooling effect, create conditions where the body transitions seamlessly into recovery mode.

Light is another crucial factor. Human biology is entrained to the rising and setting of the sun, with darkness stimulating melatonin release and signaling the brain to initiate sleep. Artificial light, particularly in the blue spectrum emitted by screens, disrupts this rhythm by tricking the brain into perceiving daylight. Darkness protocols—eliminating or reducing exposure to light in the hours before bed, using blackout curtains, or even employing sleep masks—restore the natural cues that govern circadian rhythms. For athletes traveling across time zones or maintaining irregular schedules, these protocols are invaluable for re-establishing biological alignment. In environments of true darkness, melatonin flows more freely, deepening both the onset and maintenance of sleep cycles.

Beyond environmental cues, sound can also be engineered to enhance recovery. Binaural beats, which involve presenting slightly different frequencies to each ear, create a perceptual beat frequency in the brain that can entrain neural activity. Frequencies in the delta range encourage slow-wave activity, effectively nudging the brain toward deeper sleep states. Similarly, pink noise—sound with equal energy across octaves, such as the steady rhythm of rainfall—smooths out environmental disturbances and has been shown to increase the proportion of deep sleep by as much as 25 to 35 percent. These auditory tools do not replace the body's natural processes but augment them, providing a gentle scaffold that reinforces the descent into restorative cycles.

Sleep engineering also extends to deliberate daytime rest. Strategic napping is a practice embraced by many professional athletes, yet often misunderstood by the general population. The body responds differently to short versus long naps, and each has its place in recovery architecture. A twenty-minute power nap targets light sleep stages, providing a burst of alertness and reaction speed without leaving the grogginess associated with sleep inertia. These brief naps are particularly effective for athletes who require sharpness in skill-based sports or for individuals facing long days with multiple training or work demands. In contrast, ninety-minute recovery naps encompass a full sleep cycle, including deep and REM stages. These naps provide true physical and neurological restoration, making them valuable after particularly demanding training sessions or competitions. By alternating between these nap strategies depending on the day's needs, recovery is no longer left to chance but woven deliberately into the rhythm of life.

The interaction between sleep and hormones underscores just how central rest is to adaptation. During deep sleep, pulses of growth hormone are released, driving protein synthesis, fat metabolism, and tissue repair. Insufficient deep sleep blunts these pulses, slowing recovery and compromising gains from training. Testosterone, another hormone critical to strength and vitality, is also regulated by sleep duration and quality. Even a single week of sleep restriction can reduce testosterone levels significantly, undermining performance. On the other hand, adequate sleep amplifies anabolic signals while keeping catabolic hormones like cortisol in check. Cortisol naturally peaks in the morning to promote wakefulness and declines at night; disrupted sleep reverses this rhythm, creating a hormonal environment hostile to recovery. By engineering sleep intentionally, athletes create a hormonal profile aligned with growth and resilience rather than depletion.

Sleep also directly influences the nervous system. Training, particularly high-intensity or skill-based, taxes the central nervous system, which governs coordination, reaction time, and fine motor control. Sleep restores neural efficiency, pruning unnecessary synaptic connections while strengthening those that are reinforced through repetition. This is why motor skills often improve after sleep, even without additional practice. A tennis player may find her serve more fluid the morning after training, or a weightlifter may experience sharper bar path control. Without adequate sleep, neural circuits remain cluttered and inefficient, dulling coordination and increasing the risk of errors or injury.

The concept of sleep debt highlights how easily recovery can unravel. Missed hours of sleep accumulate, and while the body can adapt temporarily, the debt eventually demands repayment. Performance declines, reaction times slow, immune function weakens, and injuries become more likely. Professional athletes recognize this danger, which is why they often log more hours of sleep than the average person, treating rest as seriously as training itself. For the fitness enthusiast, the lesson is clear: neglecting sleep in pursuit of more training sessions is counterproductive. True progress is not measured in hours spent under the bar but in the quality of adaptation that occurs afterward.

Practical sleep engineering requires not just knowledge but ritual. Consistency in bedtime and wake time anchors circadian rhythms, making it easier for the body to predict and prepare for sleep. Pre-sleep routines—such as dimming lights, avoiding screens, engaging in calming activities, or practicing breathwork—signal the nervous system that it is time to downshift. Nutrition also plays a role: heavy meals or stimulants late in the evening can disrupt sleep onset and quality, while a balanced pre-sleep snack of protein and slow-digesting carbohydrates can stabilize blood sugar and support overnight recovery.

Ultimately, sleep engineering is about reclaiming control over a process too often surrendered to chance. It is the recognition that recovery is not passive but active, and that sleep is the most powerful tool for orchestrating supercompensation. By aligning environment, sound, light, temperature, and routine with the body's natural rhythms, we can transform sleep from a background necessity into a deliberate performance enhancer. In doing so, we shift from a culture of overtraining and under-recovering to one where balance produces resilience, where rest is not weakness but the foundation of strength.

Sleep is the invisible training partner, the one that determines whether today's effort becomes tomorrow's growth or simply accumulates as fatigue. For those willing to engineer it with the same dedication given to workouts and nutrition, the rewards are profound: faster recovery, sharper focus, stronger adaptation, and ultimately, a body and mind aligned in the pursuit of excellence.

5.2 Active Recovery Modalities and Protocols

Recovery is not confined to sleep and rest alone. The body thrives when recovery itself is active—when movement, circulation, and deliberate interventions accelerate repair instead of waiting for time to do the work. Active recovery is about nudging the body toward balance, improving blood flow, reducing stiffness, and restoring neural calm while still promoting adaptations. It is the conscious decision to make recovery a session in itself rather than a passive gap between bouts of exertion.

One of the more innovative approaches in this area is blood flow restriction training used for recovery. Traditionally associated with hypertrophy and strength protocols, blood flow restriction can also be adapted for lighter recovery sessions. By applying controlled pressure to limbs with cuffs or bands, venous return is restricted while arterial inflow remains. When combined with very light movements or cyclical contractions, this creates a powerful signal for adaptation at low intensity. The restricted flow amplifies metabolic stress and accelerates the release of growth factors, all while sparing the joints and nervous system the strain of heavy lifting. Athletes have found that short, low-load sessions with blood flow restriction after intense days help preserve strength and speed up recovery, essentially tricking the body into responding as though it had experienced a greater challenge without adding more systemic fatigue.

Contrast therapy is another powerful modality, alternating between hot and cold exposures to influence circulation and inflammation. The principle is simple yet profound: heat dilates blood vessels and increases circulation, while cold constricts vessels and dampens inflammation. When alternated in deliberate cycles, the vascular system becomes a pump, flushing metabolic waste and ushering in fresh blood. Research suggests that a ratio of roughly three minutes of heat to one minute of cold creates an optimal balance, promoting recovery while avoiding the excessive stress of prolonged cold exposure. Infrared saunas, hot water immersion, and steam baths serve as the heat source, while ice baths or cold showers provide the cooling phase. The alternating waves of dilation and constriction teach the vascular system adaptability while reducing delayed-onset muscle soreness and improving perceived readiness for subsequent sessions.

Mobility flows bring yet another layer of active recovery, targeting not only the joints and muscles but also the fascial network and the nervous system. Fascia, the connective tissue web that links muscles, bones, and organs, relies on movement for hydration. Without varied motion, it stiffens and loses its elastic quality. Structured mobility routines—often blending yoga-inspired sequences with dynamic stretches and controlled breathing—restore hydration to fascia by encouraging the movement of interstitial fluids. The nervous system also benefits, as slow, mindful mobility work downshifts the body into a parasympathetic state, reducing tension and signaling safety. In this way, mobility flows become more than flexibility training; they are a full-spectrum recovery practice that combines structural care with neural relaxation.

The synergy of these active modalities lies in their complementarity. Blood flow restriction accelerates adaptation through metabolic stress without heavy exertion. Contrast therapy flushes the system and manages inflammation. Mobility flows recalibrate tissues and nervous system balance. Together, they create a layered architecture of recovery where each session is a step toward adaptation rather than a pause from it. This perspective transforms recovery into an intentional act, elevating it to the same importance as the workout itself.

5.3 Technology-Enhanced Recovery Tracking

While traditional recovery relies on listening to the body's signals, technology now provides the tools to measure those signals with precision. Recovery is no longer an abstract state of feeling rested or fatigued but a quantifiable condition revealed through biomarkers and real-time feedback. Technology-enhanced recovery tracking empowers athletes and everyday practitioners to align their effort with their readiness, preventing overtraining and unlocking higher levels of sustainable performance.

Heart rate variability, or HRV, sits at the forefront of this revolution. HRV measures the subtle variations in time between heartbeats, reflecting the balance between the sympathetic and parasympathetic branches of the autonomic nervous system. High variability indicates resilience and readiness, while low variability signals stress or incomplete recovery. Wearable devices now make HRV accessible daily, providing personalized readiness scores that guide training intensity. An athlete waking with suppressed HRV might swap a planned high-intensity session for mobility or technique work, preserving long-term progress by respecting the body's need for restoration. Over time, patterns in HRV offer deep insight into how training loads, sleep quality, nutrition, and emotional stress interact to shape recovery.

Continuous glucose monitoring provides another dimension of feedback, linking nutrition to recovery efficiency. Stable glucose patterns support consistent energy levels, reduce oxidative stress, and enhance nighttime recovery, while large fluctuations undermine performance and increase fatigue. Athletes using glucose monitoring can identify how specific foods or meal timings influence recovery quality, adjusting their fueling strategies to maintain metabolic balance. For example, a recovery meal that stabilizes glucose may accelerate glycogen replenishment, while avoiding late-night spikes can improve sleep depth. This data-driven approach removes guesswork and ensures that nutrition reinforces rather than disrupts recovery architecture.

Technological interventions also extend into direct recovery modalities. Infrared therapy has gained traction for its ability to penetrate tissues with light wavelengths that stimulate mitochondrial activity. By enhancing cellular energy production, infrared exposure supports tissue repair and reduces inflammation. Athletes use infrared saunas or targeted devices to accelerate recovery after demanding sessions, experiencing not only reduced soreness but also improved circulation. Similarly, pulsed electromagnetic field therapy, known as PEMF, uses electromagnetic fields to stimulate cellular regeneration. The low-frequency pulses encourage ion exchange across cell membranes, enhancing nutrient uptake and waste removal at the cellular level. These therapies create a microenvironment where cells operate at peak efficiency, effectively upgrading the foundation of recovery.

The integration of tracking and intervention creates a feedback loop. Data from HRV and glucose monitors guides choices, while therapies like infrared and PEMF accelerate the outcomes of those choices. Recovery is no longer a passive waiting period but a responsive system that adapts daily. The athlete or practitioner becomes a manager of their own physiology, equipped with tools that reveal when to push, when to rest, and when to intervene actively.

Yet technology is not an end in itself. It is a means of amplifying awareness, of translating the body's whispers into measurable signals. The ultimate goal remains the same: to align training and recovery so that supercompensation—the rebound beyond baseline—occurs consistently. When used wisely, technology enhances intuition rather than replacing it, guiding the individual toward sustainable cycles of stress and adaptation.

The fusion of active recovery protocols with technology-enhanced tracking embodies the essence of recovery architecture. One provides the methods to accelerate adaptation, the other provides the data to know when and how to apply them. Together, they form a structure where recovery is not guesswork but science, not absence of training but its silent partner. It is this architecture that transforms raw effort into refined performance, ensuring that every ounce of training investment yields the highest possible return.

Chapter 6: Mindful Movement Mastery — The Consciousness-Performance Connection

"Studies show that athletes who practice mindful movement techniques improve their reaction time by 20% and reduce injury rates by 45%."

6.1 Flow State Engineering Through Movement

The pursuit of excellence in physical performance has always been driven by a quest for efficiency: how to move faster, how to lift heavier, how to last longer. Yet beneath the metrics of speed, strength, and endurance lies another dimension of performance that is less tangible but no less transformative. This is the dimension of flow, the state where consciousness and movement merge into a seamless rhythm, where time feels suspended and action unfolds with effortless precision. Athletes across disciplines describe flow as being "in the zone," a condition where decisions are instantaneous, execution is flawless, and the body seems to know what to do before the mind catches up. Engineering this state through movement is not a matter of chance but of cultivating the conditions that make it most likely to appear.

Flow emerges at the intersection of challenge and skill. Too little challenge and the mind drifts into boredom; too much challenge and it collapses under anxiety. But when skill and challenge align, the nervous system enters a state of heightened engagement where focus narrows, feedback becomes immediate, and action flows without hesitation. This balance is the first trigger of flow, and movement is one of the most powerful ways to activate it. A martial artist sparring at just the right level of resistance, a dancer improvising within the limits of their technique, or a runner maintaining a pace that is demanding but sustainable—all find themselves immersed because the task stretches their capacity without overwhelming it. Training, therefore, must be designed not only to build strength and endurance but also to cultivate this balance, to position the body and mind at the edge of capacity where flow thrives.

Immediate feedback is another essential ingredient. The brain is constantly evaluating action against outcome, and the tighter this loop, the more engaged it becomes. Sports and practices that provide instant feedback—whether it is the bounce of a ball, the resistance of an opponent, or the alignment of a posture—naturally guide attention into the present moment. Flow engineering through movement requires environments where feedback is unavoidable and transparent. Video games, despite being digital, demonstrate this principle clearly: the instant correlation between action and response keeps players immersed for hours. Physical training can borrow this same structure, using tools such as resistance bands, unstable surfaces, or partner drills that provide constant feedback to refine technique. The point is not perfection but immersion, creating a space where every action generates a clear, interpretable result that keeps awareness tethered to the moment.

Vision plays a crucial role in this immersion. The way we use our eyes shapes the state of our nervous system. Narrow, focused vision often activates stress responses, preparing the body for fight-or-flight reactions. Peripheral vision, by contrast, engages the parasympathetic system, promoting calm awareness. Athletes who train their peripheral vision expand their field of awareness, allowing them to perceive opportunities and threats without the tunnel vision that leads to errors or injury. Soft focus, where the eyes take in the entire field rather than locking onto a single point, is a practical way to cultivate this state. A basketball player scanning the court, a surfer reading the movement of waves, or a cyclist monitoring the road ahead all benefit from this expanded awareness. Training can incorporate simple drills, such as maintaining peripheral awareness during agility work, or practicing soft focus in balance exercises. Over time, this visual conditioning becomes a gateway to flow, allowing the athlete to remain relaxed yet responsive, engaged yet expansive.

Flow is not reserved for long, intense sessions. Micro-flow practices—short, intentional periods of mindful movement—bring the benefits of this state into daily life. Two-minute movement meditations scattered throughout the day recalibrate both body and mind, serving as miniature portals into presence. These may take the form of slow, deliberate breathing combined with gentle stretches, mindful walking where attention is placed fully on the rhythm of steps, or simple bodyweight sequences performed with undivided focus. While brief, these micro-practices condition the nervous system to access flow more readily, making it a familiar state rather than a rare occurrence. By stringing together moments of micro-flow, the practitioner builds a baseline of awareness and composure that carries into more demanding performance contexts.

The science of flow reveals its physiological underpinnings. During flow states, the brain enters a pattern of transient hypofrontality, where activity in the prefrontal cortex—the area responsible for self-criticism and time awareness—diminishes. This quieting of self-consciousness allows action to unfold without hesitation. Neurochemicals such as dopamine, norepinephrine, and endorphins surge, sharpening focus, enhancing mood, and reducing the perception of pain. These changes not only improve immediate performance but also accelerate learning, as the brain consolidates skills more effectively when bathed in these neurochemical environments. Thus, flow is not just a subjective experience but a biological upgrade, a state where the body and mind are optimized for both execution and adaptation.

Engineering flow through movement requires deliberate attention to preparation. The body must be primed, but not overtaxed; the environment must provide feedback, but not distraction; the mind must be challenged, but not overwhelmed. Routines that begin with breath awareness, transition into warm-ups that gradually escalate challenge, and then move into skill-based practice create the scaffolding for flow. The practitioner enters a state where every variable aligns, where the noise of life recedes and only the task remains. When repeated, this pattern teaches the nervous system to recognize and re-enter flow more easily, making it less a stroke of luck and more a skill that can be cultivated.

The value of flow state engineering is not confined to athletes. In daily life, the same principles enhance productivity, creativity, and resilience. A professional preparing a presentation, an artist at the easel, or a student solving complex problems can all benefit from the balance of skill and challenge, the immediacy of feedback, and the expansion of awareness. Movement serves as an accessible gateway to these states because it engages the whole organism—body, breath, and mind—in synchronized action. Once learned through movement, the ability to enter flow becomes transferable to other domains, creating a foundation for excellence across the spectrum of human activity.

The injury-reducing power of flow highlights its practical importance. When immersed in the present, the body responds more efficiently to changes in environment, reducing missteps, slips, and poor mechanics. Athletes who cultivate flow through mindful movement make fewer errors under pressure because their awareness is both expansive and immediate. They feel the nuances of their body's alignment and adjust before strain becomes injury. They perceive shifts in opponents or environments before reaction becomes desperation. Flow, therefore, is not only about performance enhancement but also about resilience, a natural safeguard against the risks of physical exertion.

In the end, flow state engineering through movement is about aligning consciousness with the body's natural capacity for rhythm, awareness, and adaptability. It is about dissolving the artificial separation between mind and muscle, thought and action. It is about creating conditions where the body feels weightless, time feels suspended, and performance feels effortless. This is not mysticism but biology, not chance but design. By deliberately cultivating the triggers of flow—balancing challenge with skill, engaging feedback loops, expanding vision, and practicing micro-flow—we learn to live and perform in the zone more often, not as visitors but as residents.

Flow is the art of being fully alive in movement, and its cultivation is perhaps the most profound expression of fine fitness. It is where body, fuel, and consciousness converge, where performance transcends mechanics and becomes artistry. To engineer flow through movement is to rediscover the human body not only as a machine of muscle and bone but as an instrument of awareness, capable of playing the symphony of life with precision, rhythm, and grace.

6.2 Somatic Intelligence and Body Mapping

Mindful movement begins with a simple truth: you cannot master what you cannot feel. Somatic intelligence, the capacity to sense, interpret, and guide the body's internal signals, is the cornerstone of conscious performance. Many people live detached from their bodies, noticing them only when pain emerges or fatigue overwhelms. Yet elite performers cultivate a constant dialogue with their physiology, scanning for tension, adjusting posture, and detecting the smallest inefficiencies before they magnify into limitations. This level of body mapping does not arise from force or willpower but from refined awareness, a practice as much neurological as it is physical.

Interoceptive accuracy—the ability to sense internal states—can be trained much like strength or endurance. Body scanning practices invite attention to move systematically through muscles, joints, and organs, noticing sensations without judgment. Lying on the floor and directing focus from the tips of the toes to the crown of the head, an athlete might discover subtle asymmetries: a shoulder that feels heavier, a hip that resists contact with the ground, a breath that shortens when awareness arrives in the chest. These signals, once invisible, become a map of tension and release. Guided by this map, one can then practice deliberate relaxation, releasing unnecessary contractions and allowing energy to flow more freely. The nervous system, once accustomed to holding unconscious bracing patterns, begins to reset, opening space for fluidity of movement.

Beyond internal scanning, somatic intelligence extends into kinesthetic awareness, the felt sense of movement through space. The Feldenkrais method and the Alexander technique, though distinct in practice, both emphasize this principle: movement is most efficient when guided by awareness rather than rigid correction. Feldenkrais lessons often involve slow, exploratory motions that reveal alternative movement pathways, teaching the nervous system options beyond habitual patterns. The Alexander technique, meanwhile, focuses on undoing unnecessary effort, particularly in the neck and spine, so that natural alignment can emerge. Both approaches reject the idea of imposing ideal form from the outside, instead cultivating the inner intelligence that allows the body to self-organize toward efficiency.

This cultivation of awareness has practical implications far beyond therapy or rehabilitation. Athletes who develop kinesthetic refinement waste less energy in compensation, move with greater economy, and reduce injury risk. A sprinter aware of subtle hip misalignment can adjust stride mechanics before pain emerges. A violinist who senses tension in the shoulders can release it before it becomes repetitive strain. In each case, awareness precedes adaptation. By training attention, the body learns to move with intelligence, precision, and grace.

Movement variability is another crucial dimension of somatic development. The body thrives on diversity of input; repeating the same patterns endlessly may build strength but also narrows adaptability. Constraints-based coaching creates environments where the body must find new solutions. A basketball player practicing with one hand tied, a dancer restricted to a small square of space, or a lifter performing with deliberately uneven loads—all encounter challenges that force exploration. Through this exploration, the nervous system expands its repertoire, mapping new pathways that can be called upon in unpredictable circumstances. Variability is not randomness but deliberate novelty, a way of stretching somatic intelligence so that movement becomes resilient under any condition.

When interoception, kinesthetic awareness, and variability converge, the body ceases to be a collection of mechanical levers and becomes an intelligent organism capable of adapting with fluidity. This is somatic mastery: the sense that the body is not an obstacle or a mystery but a trusted partner in performance. It transforms movement from effortful execution into an act of embodied awareness, where efficiency, resilience, and creativity all flow from the same source—an intimate dialogue with the self.

6.3 Breath as the Master Controller

If somatic intelligence is the map of the body, breath is the master controller of the terrain. Every system of physiology is influenced by respiration: cardiovascular function, nervous system balance, energy metabolism, and even emotional regulation. Breath is the only function that bridges conscious control and automatic rhythm. You cannot will your heart to slow directly, but by changing your breathing pattern, you influence heart rate, blood pressure, and the cascade of hormones that follow. For this reason, breath training has become a central pillar of mindful movement and performance mastery.

One of the most accessible techniques is box breathing, structured as equal-length phases of inhalation, retention, exhalation, and pause—often in counts of four. This simple rhythm creates coherence between the sympathetic and parasympathetic nervous systems, stabilizing heart rate variability and calming overactive stress responses. Practiced before training, it centers the mind; practiced after, it accelerates recovery. Box breathing serves as both anchor and regulator, a way of keeping the nervous system within a window of optimal arousal where performance is heightened without tipping into panic or fatigue.

More intense methods, such as the Wim Hof approach, harness breath to create resilience under stress. Cycles of hyperventilation followed by prolonged breath holds induce temporary hypoxia and elevated CO_2, training the body to tolerate conditions of discomfort. This practice stimulates the release of adrenaline in a controlled setting, "inoculating" the nervous system against future stress. Studies suggest that regular practice can enhance immune resilience, improve cold tolerance, and sharpen focus. For athletes, it offers a way to rehearse the stress of competition or exertion in a safe, controlled environment, building confidence in their capacity to remain calm under pressure.

Breath holds and CO2 tolerance tables provide another avenue for resilience training. Most people think they run out of oxygen during breath holding, but in truth, the urge to breathe arises from rising CO2 levels. By gradually extending tolerance to elevated CO2, practitioners retrain the chemoreceptors that trigger respiratory drive. This translates into delayed fatigue during exertion, as the body becomes comfortable with higher lactate levels and greater acidity. Freedivers rely on this adaptation to extend dives, but athletes of all kinds benefit from the same principle. A runner who tolerates CO2 more effectively can maintain pace longer before acidosis forces slowdown. A fighter who can remain calm while oxygen dips and CO2 rises will outlast an opponent in high-pressure exchanges.

Breath also acts as a gateway to mental states. Slow diaphragmatic breathing stimulates the vagus nerve, activating parasympathetic dominance and reducing anxiety. Rapid, forceful breathing activates sympathetic arousal, preparing the body for explosive action. The ability to shift between these states consciously is the essence of breath mastery. It is the art of tuning the nervous system like an instrument, raising or lowering arousal to meet the demands of the moment.

When integrated with mindful movement, breath becomes inseparable from action. A weightlifter coordinating exhalation with exertion, a yogi synchronizing breath with asana, or a swimmer aligning strokes with inhalations all demonstrate the union of respiration and performance. In these moments, breath is not an afterthought but the conductor of rhythm, the thread that ties body and mind together in flow.

Breath, like somatic intelligence, transforms training into awareness. It takes what is automatic and makes it conscious, then returns it to automatic with new refinement. In doing so, it offers mastery not only over movement but over the states of mind and body that define performance. It is at once the simplest and the most profound of tools: always available, endlessly adaptable, and capable of reshaping physiology in real time.

Chapter 7: The Hormonal Optimization Blueprint

"Optimizing just 4 key hormones can increase muscle growth by 40%, accelerate fat loss by 60%, and improve energy levels by 80%."

7.1 Testosterone and Growth Hormone Maximization

Hormones are the silent architects of performance. They dictate how the body partitions energy, how efficiently it builds muscle, how rapidly it recovers, and even how motivated a person feels to train in the first place. Among the many chemical messengers circulating through the bloodstream, two stand out as pivotal for physical development and resilience: testosterone and growth hormone. When cultivated naturally through training, nutrition, and lifestyle, these hormones unlock levels of vitality and adaptation that no supplement or shortcut can replicate.

Testosterone is often misunderstood as merely the "muscle hormone," but its influence is broader. It enhances protein synthesis, drives red blood cell production, supports bone density, and fuels confidence and drive. Growth hormone, secreted in pulses throughout the day but peaking at night, stimulates tissue repair, fat metabolism, and collagen synthesis, making it equally essential for both performance and recovery. Together, these hormones form a powerful partnership: testosterone directs the building of muscle and strength, while growth hormone ensures tissues regenerate and energy reserves are mobilized. To maximize them is not to chase vanity but to build a foundation for long-term health and capacity.

One of the most reliable natural triggers of testosterone production is mechanical tension imposed through compound movement patterns. Exercises that recruit multiple large muscle groups simultaneously—such as squats, deadlifts, pull-ups, and presses—create hormonal responses far greater than isolation exercises. When the body senses the demand to coordinate vast networks of muscles under heavy load, it responds by releasing more testosterone to drive adaptation. The nervous system, taxed by the complexity of these movements, amplifies the signal, recruiting motor units and triggering endocrine cascades. Training with intensity, focusing on progressive overload, and emphasizing these foundational patterns establishes an internal environment where testosterone thrives. The goal is not reckless loading but consistent, challenging effort where the body perceives a legitimate demand to become stronger.

Growth hormone responds differently, thriving not only on resistance training but also on short, high-intensity bursts of cardiovascular work. Sprint intervals, for example, are one of the most potent natural stimulators of growth hormone, with increases of 400 to 700 percent documented in the hours following such efforts. The intensity of a sprint—whether on a track, bike, or rower—forces the body into oxygen debt, triggering a cascade of metabolic stress that signals the pituitary gland to release growth hormone in abundance. Unlike long-duration steady-state cardio, which can sometimes suppress anabolic hormones when performed excessively, sprint intervals combine efficiency with endocrine stimulation. Just a handful of brief all-out efforts, followed by sufficient recovery, can rival the hormonal impact of far longer sessions. For athletes, these protocols provide not only metabolic conditioning but also a direct boost to recovery and tissue repair.

Nutrition plays a decisive role in supporting these hormonal surges. Testosterone synthesis depends on adequate levels of vitamin D, zinc, and magnesium, three micronutrients frequently deficient in modern populations. Vitamin D functions more like a steroid hormone than a vitamin, influencing testosterone production at the cellular level. Sun exposure remains the most powerful natural source, but in its absence, supplementation ensures adequate levels. Zinc is directly involved in enzymatic reactions that convert cholesterol into testosterone, while magnesium supports both the activation of vitamin D and the regulation of free testosterone by influencing binding proteins in the blood. Deficiency in any of these nutrients constrains hormonal production, no matter how effective the training stimulus. Optimization, by contrast, amplifies the body's natural output, ensuring that each rep, sprint, and recovery phase yields its fullest potential.

Sleep, too, cannot be separated from hormonal optimization. Growth hormone secretion occurs primarily during deep slow-wave sleep, meaning that disruptions in sleep architecture diminish recovery regardless of training quality. Testosterone levels follow a similar pattern, peaking during the early hours of sleep and tapering off during the day. A single night of inadequate rest can drop testosterone levels by double-digit percentages, while chronic deprivation leads to a cumulative suppression that undermines progress. Engineering sleep environments—through temperature, darkness, and routine—

becomes as crucial to hormonal health as any training or supplement.

Beyond the physiological, lifestyle choices exert powerful influence. Chronic stress elevates cortisol, the body's primary stress hormone, which directly antagonizes both testosterone and growth hormone. Prolonged elevation of cortisol not only blunts anabolic signals but also increases fat storage and erodes lean tissue. Stress management practices—breathwork, mindfulness, time in nature, and balanced scheduling—are not luxuries but necessities for anyone serious about maximizing hormonal health. The body is not fooled by supplements or stimulants; it responds to the signals of environment and behavior.

The interplay between training, nutrition, and lifestyle forms a holistic blueprint. Compound lifts and sprint intervals create the initial hormonal surges. Nutritional optimization ensures that raw materials for hormone synthesis are abundant. Sleep provides the nightly stage for hormonal pulses to shape adaptation. Stress regulation prevents catabolic interference. Together, these pillars create a hormonal environment where muscle growth accelerates, fat loss becomes more efficient, and energy levels rise naturally.

The rewards of maximizing testosterone and growth hormone extend beyond the gym. Stronger muscles support joint health and functional movement. Higher bone density reduces the risk of fractures later in life. Enhanced collagen synthesis strengthens tendons and ligaments, reducing injury risk. Improved fat metabolism supports cardiovascular health and energy stability. Elevated red blood cell counts improve oxygen delivery, sharpening endurance. Even mood and cognition benefit, as these hormones influence neurotransmitter balance, motivation, and resilience against depression. What begins as a pursuit of performance becomes, at its core, a pursuit of longevity and vitality.

It is easy to mistake hormonal optimization as a pursuit reserved for professional athletes, but it is deeply relevant to anyone seeking to live fully. The declines in testosterone and growth hormone that accompany aging are not inevitable sentences of weakness and fatigue; they are signals to re-align training, nutrition, and recovery. By respecting the body's natural pathways and amplifying them through deliberate practice, men and women alike can sustain vitality well into later decades.

Ultimately, testosterone and growth hormone are not magic bullets but amplifiers of effort. They respond to the signals we send through challenge, nourishment, rest, and balance. When cultivated, they transform the return on investment from training, making every hour of effort yield greater rewards. To maximize them is not to chase shortcuts but to embrace the fundamental truth of biology: the body adapts best when its chemical messengers are aligned with its physical demands.

The hormonal optimization blueprint begins here, with the recognition that the foundation of strength, recovery, and energy is not in supplements or extremes, but in the intelligent engineering of the very hormones that evolution designed for adaptation. Testosterone and growth hormone, when nurtured, open the door to a level of performance that feels not only stronger and faster but more deeply alive.

7.2 Cortisol Management and Stress Adaptation

Cortisol is often painted as the villain of performance, the catabolic hormone that undermines muscle growth and fuels fat storage. Yet like all hormones, it is not inherently harmful but context dependent. Cortisol is essential for mobilizing energy during stress, regulating blood sugar, and sharpening focus in moments of urgency. The problem arises when cortisol remains chronically elevated, eroding recovery, impairing sleep, and creating a biochemical environment that blunts adaptation. Managing cortisol is therefore not about eliminating it but about restoring its natural rhythm, using both physiological strategies and lifestyle practices to cultivate resilience.

One of the most powerful ways to reshape cortisol response is through hormetic stress—controlled exposures that challenge the body in short, deliberate doses, teaching it to adapt more effectively. Cold exposure exemplifies this principle. Immersion in icy water or even a brief cold shower triggers an acute stress response, elevating cortisol and adrenaline in the moment but leading to long-term reductions in baseline levels. The repeated practice of cold immersion trains the nervous system to recover more quickly from stress, enhancing both resilience and mental toughness. Heat therapy works on similar principles. Time spent in saunas elevates heart rate, stimulates heat shock proteins, and creates a temporary stress environment. Yet when used consistently, heat therapy lowers chronic cortisol, improves cardiovascular efficiency, and supports recovery. The alternating use of heat and cold teaches the endocrine system adaptability, providing a reset that blunts the harmful effects of unrelenting modern stress.

Adaptogens provide another layer of modulation. Substances like ashwagandha, rhodiola, and holy basil influence the hypothalamic-pituitary-adrenal axis, smoothing out cortisol spikes and enhancing the body's ability to return to baseline. Timing is critical. Taken in the morning, adaptogens can support natural cortisol rhythms, reinforcing the peak that helps drive wakefulness and focus. Taken later in the day, they may reduce excessive evening levels, creating the hormonal environment necessary for restful sleep. The goal is not suppression but balance—ensuring that cortisol rises when it should and declines when the day winds down.

Nature itself offers one of the most accessible and effective cortisol regulators. Studies on forest bathing, the Japanese practice of immersing oneself in wooded environments, demonstrate reductions in cortisol levels of up to 50 percent after even short exposure. The mechanisms are multifaceted: reduced sensory overload, increased parasympathetic activity, and the influence of phytoncides, organic compounds emitted by plants that interact with the nervous system. Unlike synthetic interventions, nature provides a holistic recalibration, reminding the body of rhythms it evolved to recognize. Regular exposure to natural environments counters the chronic stimulation of urban life, anchoring cortisol in patterns aligned with rest, activity, and recovery.

Cortisol management is ultimately about rhythm. Peaks are natural and beneficial, providing the drive to act. Valleys are equally necessary, allowing for rest and regeneration. The modern challenge is that many people remain stuck in peaks, never allowing the system to reset. Through hormetic stress, adaptogenic support, and reconnection with nature, the endocrine system can be taught once again to oscillate. The result is not only improved recovery and physical adaptation but also enhanced mood, clearer cognition, and greater resilience to the inevitable pressures of life.

7.3 Thyroid and Metabolic Hormone Optimization

If testosterone and growth hormone dictate anabolic drive, and cortisol represents the stress axis, the thyroid is the conductor of metabolic rhythm. Thyroid hormones regulate how quickly the body converts fuel into energy, how efficiently calories are burned, and how responsive tissues remain to training stimuli. Optimizing thyroid function is not simply about weight management but about sustaining the metabolic fire that supports performance, recovery, and vitality.

The thyroid gland relies on key nutritional inputs to produce its primary hormones, T4 and T3. Selenium is required for the enzymes that convert T4 into the more active T3. Iodine provides the raw material for thyroid hormone synthesis. Tyrosine, an amino acid derived from dietary protein, forms the backbone of these molecules. Deficiency in any of these nutrients creates bottlenecks that slow metabolism, leaving individuals fatigued, unable to lose fat efficiently, and more prone to injury due to slower recovery. Ensuring adequate intake of these nutrients, whether through whole foods like seaweed, nuts, and protein sources or through targeted supplementation, provides the thyroid with the tools it needs to sustain metabolic output.

Another critical dimension of thyroid health involves the management of reverse T3. Under conditions of prolonged calorie restriction or stress, the body converts T4 not into active T3 but into reverse T3, an inactive form that blunts metabolic rate as a protective mechanism. This evolutionary safeguard prevents starvation but in the modern fitness context, it can stall fat loss and undermine training progress. Managing reverse T3 requires careful balance: sufficient calorie intake to avoid signaling famine, appropriate recovery to reduce stress load, and strategic use of refeed days where carbohydrate intake is deliberately increased to reassure the body that energy is abundant. These strategies preserve metabolic rate during fat loss phases, ensuring that the thyroid remains responsive and adaptation continues.

Thyroid function is closely linked to the regulation of leptin and ghrelin, the hormones governing appetite and satiety. Leptin, secreted by fat cells, signals energy sufficiency to the brain, while ghrelin, produced in the stomach, stimulates hunger. Prolonged dieting reduces leptin and elevates ghrelin, driving hunger and slowing metabolism. Strategic refeeds—periods of increased carbohydrate intake—temporarily boost leptin, resetting the system and preventing the metabolic slowdown that often accompanies long-term restriction. Intermittent fasting, when applied judiciously, can also improve leptin sensitivity, teaching the body to respond more efficiently to satiety signals. The manipulation of these hormones allows for fat loss without the spiral into metabolic suppression, preserving energy, mood, and performance throughout the process.

Optimizing thyroid and metabolic hormones requires more than isolated tactics. It demands a recognition of balance: providing nutrients for synthesis, avoiding extremes that trigger protective slowdowns, and cycling intake to reassure the body that it is safe to maintain output. When these systems are aligned, the body becomes metabolically flexible, capable of shifting between fuel sources efficiently, burning fat without sacrificing muscle, and sustaining high energy levels throughout the day.

The integration of thyroid health with cortisol management reveals the full scope of the hormonal optimization blueprint. When cortisol is balanced, stress no longer suppresses thyroid output. When thyroid function is optimized, metabolism remains robust even during fat loss. When leptin and ghrelin are managed, appetite supports rather than sabotages progress. Together, these systems ensure that the body operates not in survival mode but in performance mode, primed for adaptation, growth, and vitality.

Hormones, after all, are not independent actors. They are part of a symphony, where testosterone, growth hormone, cortisol, and thyroid hormones all influence one another. To optimize one while neglecting the others is to tune a single instrument while leaving the orchestra out of harmony. By addressing each system deliberately, through training, nutrition, stress management, and lifestyle design, the entire symphony can be brought into alignment. The result is a body that grows stronger, recovers faster, and performs with energy that feels limitless.

Chapter 8: Advanced Training Periodization — The Art of Strategic Programming

"Olympic athletes change their training variables every 2-3 weeks, while most gym-goers haven't changed their routine in 2-3 years."

8.1 Undulating Periodization for Continuous Adaptation

Adaptation is the essence of training, but the body is a master of efficiency. It responds to stress initially with dramatic improvements, but as weeks pass, the same routine loses its impact. What once felt challenging becomes manageable, then monotonous, and eventually stagnates. This is the trap of linear progressions—the belief that one can endlessly add weight, volume, or intensity without variation. While this approach may work for beginners, it eventually collapses under the reality of physiology. The solution lies in advanced periodization, a strategic manipulation of variables that keeps the body guessing, ensures recovery, and allows progress to unfold over months and years rather than weeks.

Undulating periodization is one of the most effective approaches to this problem. Rather than progressing in a straight line, it introduces variation within shorter cycles, changing intensity, volume, and even exercise focus on a daily or weekly basis. The body, confronted with constantly shifting demands, is unable to settle into complacency. The nervous system remains engaged, hormonal responses remain sharp, and performance continues to rise. Research has consistently demonstrated that undulating models, particularly daily undulating periodization (DUP), produce greater strength gains—up to fifteen percent higher—compared to linear approaches.

Daily undulating periodization structures training so that different qualities are emphasized on different days of the week. A lifter might train strength on Monday with heavy, low-repetition sets, hypertrophy on Wednesday with moderate loads and higher volume, and power on Friday with explosive, lighter movements. Each quality feeds into the others: the strength day builds raw force, the hypertrophy day expands muscle cross-sectional area, and the power day teaches rapid recruitment of motor units. By the end of the week, the athlete has touched on multiple adaptations without overtaxing any single pathway. The constant variation keeps muscles and the nervous system primed, while the cyclical rotation prevents the monotony that often erodes motivation.

Block periodization offers another strategic layer, particularly for those peaking for events or goals. Instead of balancing all qualities within the same week, block models concentrate on one quality for a set period, often four to six weeks, before shifting to the next. For example, an athlete might begin with a block focused on hypertrophy, laying the muscular foundation with higher volume. This is followed by a strength block, where heavier loads teach those larger muscles to produce maximal force. Finally, a peaking block emphasizes power or endurance, depending on the demands of the event. The sequencing of blocks is deliberate, each building on the adaptations of the previous. This model ensures that the athlete arrives at competition—or at a personal milestone—in peak condition, with all systems aligned for maximal output.

Conjugate systems blend the strengths of both approaches by training multiple qualities simultaneously, but in a more structured manner than undulating models alone. Originating in powerlifting circles, the conjugate method divides training into sessions targeting maximal effort, dynamic effort, and repetition effort. Maximal effort sessions push the nervous system to recruit its highest threshold motor units. Dynamic effort sessions emphasize speed and explosive movement with moderate loads. Repetition effort sessions provide hypertrophy and muscular endurance. Rotating exercises within these categories prevents stagnation while ensuring that every facet of performance—strength, speed, and size—is addressed consistently. Over time, the conjugate approach develops athletes who are not only strong but also powerful, durable, and adaptable.

The underlying philosophy of undulating, block, and conjugate systems is the same: the body thrives on variation when structured intelligently. Too much randomness leads to chaos, while too much rigidity leads to stagnation. Periodization provides the artful middle ground, a balance between planned progression and adaptive stimulus. Olympic athletes embody this principle, adjusting training every two to three weeks to align with competition schedules and recovery demands. The average gym-goer, by contrast, often repeats the same program for years, wondering why progress stalls. The difference lies not in genetics or equipment but in the sophistication of programming.

Undulating periodization also acknowledges the psychological dimension of training. Constantly repeating the same rep schemes and loads dulls motivation, while the novelty of changing variables rekindles engagement. Athletes often find themselves looking forward to the variety of their programs, knowing that each day offers a different challenge. This psychological freshness translates into physiological benefits, as effort remains high and compliance improves. The best program is not only the one that works physiologically but also the one that the athlete is excited to follow consistently.

The art of strategic programming lies in weaving these models together based on context. A beginner may thrive on simple linear progressions, but as adaptation slows, undulating variation provides the spark to continue. An athlete preparing for competition may transition into block structures, each carefully sequenced toward a peak. A strength enthusiast seeking balance may adopt a conjugate approach, ensuring no quality is neglected. The practitioner, whether coach or individual, becomes an architect, designing training not as a static plan but as a living process that evolves in response to progress, goals, and feedback.

Recovery is woven into these models deliberately. Undulating systems balance heavy and light days to allow neural and muscular systems to rebound. Block models incorporate deload weeks to consolidate adaptations. Conjugate methods rotate exercises to reduce overuse and distribute stress across tissues. This built-in recovery is what makes periodization sustainable. Without it, training becomes a cycle of overreaching and breakdown. With it, training becomes a lifelong pursuit where progress continues without interruption.

At the heart of undulating periodization is respect for the body's adaptability. The body is designed to respond to challenges, but it resists monotony. By varying intensity, volume, and focus across days and weeks, undulating systems speak directly to this truth. They keep the body guessing, the mind engaged, and the path of progress open. Whether the goal is strength, endurance, aesthetics, or performance, the principle remains the same: continuous adaptation requires continuous variation.

Strategic programming, then, is not about rigid adherence to a template but about understanding the principles that drive adaptation and applying them artfully. Just as a composer uses rhythm and harmony to create music, a coach or athlete uses periodization to create progression. Undulating models provide the rhythm, block models provide the structure, and conjugate systems provide the harmony. Together, they transform training from repetition into evolution, from routine into mastery.

In the end, the art of periodization is the art of anticipation: anticipating plateaus before they occur, anticipating recovery needs before fatigue accumulates, and anticipating goals before they arrive. Undulating periodization, with its dynamic variation, offers one of the most powerful tools for this anticipation, ensuring that adaptation never stalls and that every session contributes to a broader arc of progress. For those willing to embrace change and complexity, it provides not only greater strength gains but also a path toward sustainable, lifelong fitness.

8.2 Autoregulation and Biofeedback Training

Even the most sophisticated training plan cannot predict every variable of human performance. Stress at work, disrupted sleep, illness, or even subtle hormonal fluctuations can shift readiness on any given day. A program that demands maximal intensity regardless of the athlete's state risks not only poor performance but also injury and burnout. Autoregulation addresses this challenge by creating flexibility within structure, allowing training to adapt to the individual's readiness in real time rather than forcing the individual to conform to the plan.

One of the most common autoregulatory tools is the use of perceived exertion as a guide. The rate of perceived exertion, or RPE, asks the athlete to evaluate how demanding a set or session feels on a scale of effort, typically from one to ten. Instead of prescribing fixed weights or repetitions, training might be designed around hitting an RPE of eight, which implies leaving two repetitions in reserve. This approach allows for adjustment: on days of high readiness, the athlete may push heavier loads while still staying within the prescribed exertion zone; on days of fatigue, lighter weights may be chosen to match the same effort level. Over time, this practice cultivates self-awareness and reduces the gap between perceived effort and actual performance capacity, making athletes more attuned to their bodies.

Velocity-based autoregulation offers another layer of precision. By measuring the speed of barbell movements, often with specialized sensors or even smartphone applications, athletes gain objective data on how their nervous system is performing that day. If bar speed slows dramatically at a given weight, it signals fatigue or diminished readiness, prompting adjustments.

Conversely, if bar speed is higher than usual, it indicates an opportunity to push beyond planned loads. This method transforms training into a responsive dialogue with the nervous system, aligning effort not with arbitrary numbers but with real-time performance indicators. The focus shifts from hitting specific weights to maintaining the intent to move explosively, ensuring that adaptation remains targeted toward power and strength rather than fatigue.

The philosophy of autoregulation is not chaos but structured flexibility. Training templates remain in place, but they are designed to flex with conditions. Instead of prescribing exact percentages of a maximum lift for every session, ranges are provided, and the athlete chooses within that range based on readiness markers. Warm-ups, movement quality, bar speed, and subjective energy all inform these choices. Over weeks and months, the plan remains coherent, but within each day it breathes, adjusting to align with the complex reality of human performance.

Biofeedback extends beyond the gym into physiological monitoring. Tools that track heart rate variability, sleep quality, and resting heart rate offer objective insights into recovery and readiness. An athlete waking with suppressed heart rate variability may opt for a mobility and technique session rather than maximal lifting. Another waking with unusually high bar speed in warm-ups might seize the opportunity to push intensity. In both cases, biofeedback transforms training into a partnership with the body rather than a battle against it.

The power of autoregulation lies not only in performance optimization but also in longevity. By respecting daily fluctuations, athletes avoid the chronic accumulation of fatigue that leads to overtraining. Instead of grinding through suboptimal sessions that provide little benefit, energy is allocated where it yields the greatest return. Over years, this means fewer injuries, more consistent progress, and a body that thrives on training rather than breaking down under it.

8.3 Deload Strategies and Planned Overreaching

No matter how intelligently programmed, training creates fatigue. The nervous system, muscles, and connective tissues all accumulate stress that cannot be endlessly pushed upward. Without periodic relief, adaptation stalls and performance plateaus. Deloading is the practice of deliberately reducing training stress to allow recovery while preserving adaptations. Far from being a break or a step backward, deloads are the hidden engine of long-term progress, the moments when the body consolidates gains and prepares for the next cycle.

Deloads can be passive, involving complete rest, but more often they are active, preserving movement patterns and neural adaptations while reducing overall volume and intensity. An athlete might maintain key lifts but cut sets in half, or perform accessory work at lower loads and higher control. This approach prevents detraining while giving tissues a chance to heal and the nervous system a chance to recalibrate. Active deloads are particularly effective because they maintain rhythm and skill without compounding fatigue. When training resumes, athletes often find themselves stronger, faster, and more resilient, evidence of the supercompensation effect at work.

Planned overreaching is the deliberate counterpart to deloading, where training stress is intentionally pushed beyond normal levels for a short period. For one to two weeks, volume and intensity may be increased dramatically, creating a temporary state of fatigue. Performance often dips during this time, but when followed by a deload, the rebound can be dramatic. This method is commonly used by competitive athletes in the lead-up to major events, ensuring that they peak precisely when it matters most. The art lies in timing: too much overreaching without adequate recovery leads to burnout, while too little fails to generate meaningful adaptation. When executed correctly, however, functional overreaching primes the body for breakthroughs that steady training alone cannot provide.

Tapering is another critical strategy for competition preparation. In the final days or weeks before an event, training volume is systematically reduced while intensity may be maintained or slightly elevated. The purpose is to shed accumulated fatigue while preserving the sharpness of neural adaptations. Distance runners, powerlifters, and swimmers alike use tapering to arrive at the starting line rested yet primed, with physiological systems fully recovered and psychological confidence high. The taper is a fine balance: reduce too much and detraining begins; reduce too little and fatigue lingers into competition. Mastering this balance is one of the hallmarks of elite coaching.

The interplay between planned overreaching, tapering, and deloading forms the rhythm of long-term periodization. Stress is applied, fatigue accumulates, recovery is permitted, and performance rebounds at a higher level than before. This is the essence of supercompensation, the principle that underlies all adaptive training. Without recovery phases, training is simply stress. With them, training becomes transformation.

For the average fitness enthusiast, deloads may seem unnecessary, but in reality, they are often the missing piece. Many gym-goers plateau not because their programs are flawed but because they never allow recovery to catch up. By strategically incorporating lighter weeks, even non-competitive individuals can break through stagnation and rediscover progress. For athletes, these strategies are non-negotiable, the difference between peaking on the day of competition or falling short despite months of preparation.

Ultimately, deloading and overreaching represent two sides of the same coin: the push and the pause, the acceleration and the brake. Together, they allow training to oscillate in harmony with the body's capacity, ensuring that growth continues without collapse. They remind us that progress is not a straight line but a wave, one that rises higher with each cycle of stress and recovery.

Chapter 9: Environmental Training Optimization

"Training at different temperatures, altitudes, and environments can improve performance by 25% more than conventional gym training alone."

9.1 Altitude Training and Hypoxic Conditioning

Human beings evolved in diverse environments, from sea level coasts to high mountain ranges. For millennia, bodies adapted to oxygen scarcity at altitude, to the strain of thin air, and to the challenge of surviving where every breath demanded more effort. In modern performance science, this adaptation has become a tool rather than a threat. By simulating or directly exposing the body to low-oxygen environments, athletes can unlock changes in blood chemistry, muscle metabolism, and cellular efficiency that traditional training cannot achieve. Altitude training and hypoxic conditioning have become essential methods for those who seek to extend endurance, accelerate recovery, and build resilience in ways conventional gym environments rarely allow.

At the core of altitude training is the body's response to reduced oxygen availability. At higher elevations, air pressure decreases, lowering the amount of oxygen available for each breath. This hypoxic stress forces the body to adapt by producing more erythropoietin (EPO), a hormone that stimulates red blood cell production. With more red blood cells, the blood carries greater volumes of oxygen, enhancing endurance when the athlete returns to sea level. These adaptations extend beyond oxygen transport. Mitochondria, the energy-producing organelles in cells, also become more efficient under hypoxic stress, enabling greater ATP production with less oxygen. The result is a body that learns to function optimally in scarcity, and once returned to abundance, operates at an elevated level of performance.

For athletes who cannot live permanently at high altitude, simulation has become an accessible alternative. Breath-hold training is one of the simplest yet most profound methods. By holding the breath during exercise or recovery, oxygen availability decreases while carbon dioxide rises, mimicking the environment of altitude. Over time, the body adapts by improving oxygen utilization and increasing tolerance to elevated CO_2. This training teaches both the muscles and the nervous system to endure the discomfort of hypoxia, developing resilience that translates into longer endurance, faster recovery, and sharper focus under strain. Hypoxic masks, which restrict airflow to simulate altitude conditions, extend this principle. Though not identical to true altitude, they condition respiratory muscles, elevate CO_2 tolerance, and challenge oxygen delivery in ways that sharpen performance.

One of the most refined strategies in altitude training is known as "Live High, Train Low." This approach capitalizes on the adaptations of high-altitude living while preserving the intensity possible at lower elevations. By living or sleeping in hypoxic environments—whether at natural elevation or in simulated chambers—athletes stimulate red blood cell production and mitochondrial adaptations. By descending to lower altitudes for training sessions, they maintain the ability to perform at higher intensities that thin air would otherwise prevent. This duality ensures that endurance is enhanced without sacrificing power or speed. For urban athletes, technological advances now make this strategy accessible through hypoxic tents, altitude simulation rooms, or intermittent use of masks and chambers that replicate the oxygen conditions of high elevations. The principle remains the same: create adaptation in recovery environments while preserving maximal output in training environments.

Intermittent hypoxic training (IHT) represents another sophisticated method, alternating short exposures to hypoxia with periods of normal oxygen. These cycles trigger cellular signaling pathways that increase mitochondrial density and efficiency. Rather than relying solely on structural changes like more red blood cells, IHT conditions the metabolic machinery of muscles themselves. The mitochondria learn to thrive under limited oxygen, producing energy with greater efficiency and resilience. This cellular adaptation is especially powerful for endurance athletes, but it also benefits anyone who seeks to improve metabolic flexibility, fat utilization, and recovery capacity. By weaving hypoxic intervals into regular training—whether through breath-holds, mask sessions, or chamber exposure—athletes create a metabolic resilience that persists long after oxygen availability is restored.

The benefits of hypoxic conditioning extend beyond endurance. Short bursts of hypoxic stress stimulate angiogenesis, the formation of new capillaries that deliver blood to muscle fibers. More capillaries mean more efficient nutrient and oxygen delivery, enhancing both power and recovery. Hypoxia also triggers the release of vascular endothelial growth factor (VEGF) and other signaling molecules that promote cellular regeneration.

These changes strengthen tissues against fatigue and injury, making hypoxic training as much about resilience as about stamina.

Mental toughness is another hidden benefit. Training in hypoxic states is uncomfortable. Breathlessness, rising CO_2, and the urge to stop press against the limits of tolerance. Learning to remain calm under these conditions cultivates psychological resilience that extends into competition and daily life. Athletes who master hypoxic discomfort often report greater composure under pressure, improved focus in high-stress environments, and the ability to push through fatigue without panic. The body adapts not only physiologically but psychologically, reinforcing the unity of mind and muscle in performance.

The challenge of altitude and hypoxic training lies in balance. Too much exposure without recovery risks overtraining, suppressed immune function, or excessive fatigue. Too little fails to stimulate adaptation. The art is in cycling exposure—using breath-hold protocols or intermittent mask sessions several times per week, alternating hypoxic sleep environments with high-intensity training at normal oxygen, or layering IHT into endurance programs during specific blocks of preparation. The balance ensures that the stress remains hormetic, producing adaptation rather than depletion.

Importantly, hypoxic conditioning is not reserved for elite competitors. Recreational athletes, weekend warriors, and even those pursuing fitness for health can benefit. Enhanced mitochondrial function improves metabolic health, supporting blood sugar regulation and fat oxidation. Increased capillary density supports cardiovascular efficiency and reduces the risk of chronic disease. Even the cognitive benefits are profound: hypoxic exposure stimulates neurotrophic factors that support brain health, improving clarity and resilience against age-related decline. Thus, what began as a tool for mountaineers and Olympians has relevance for anyone seeking to extend vitality.

Altitude and hypoxic training represent a powerful reminder that environment shapes adaptation as much as training itself. By stepping outside the controlled, oxygen-rich bubble of conventional gyms and deliberately challenging the body with scarcity, new layers of performance emerge. The principle is simple: when the body learns to do more with less, it thrives when resources are abundant. In this sense, hypoxic conditioning is not an exotic add-on but a central expression of fine fitness, where body, fuel, and flow converge with environment to produce transformation.

The oxygen we breathe is invisible, often taken for granted. Yet when its availability is manipulated with intention, it becomes one of the most powerful training variables. To engineer hypoxic stress is to invite the body into deeper adaptation, to awaken pathways of resilience written into our evolutionary history. In mastering these environments—whether through altitude living, breath-hold drills, or intermittent exposure—we rediscover capacities that remain dormant in the oxygen-rich safety of daily life.

9.2 Temperature Manipulation for Adaptation

Environment shapes physiology in ways that structured exercise alone cannot. Among the most powerful environmental stressors are temperature extremes, which push the body to develop resilience, adaptability, and efficiency. Heat and cold are not merely obstacles to overcome but tools to sharpen performance, expand metabolic flexibility, and enhance recovery. When used strategically, they transform ordinary training into a stimulus that reaches deeper layers of adaptation.

Heat acclimation has been studied extensively, not only in athletes who must compete in hot climates but also in those training in moderate environments who seek to broaden their capacity. Repeated exposure to elevated temperatures—whether through training sessions in the heat, sauna use, or heated environments—induces adaptations that benefit performance across all conditions. Plasma volume expands, allowing for more efficient blood flow and cooling. Sweating becomes more efficient, beginning earlier and conserving electrolytes. Heart rate at submaximal efforts decreases, while oxygen delivery improves. These adaptations do not vanish when the athlete returns to cooler conditions; instead, they carry over, providing resilience against both heat stress and normal training demands. Heat acclimation effectively raises the ceiling of endurance, allowing the same workload to feel easier and recovery to unfold more smoothly.

Cold exposure, by contrast, engages different pathways. Immersion in icy water, cold showers, or exposure to frigid air triggers a powerful cascade of metabolic and hormonal responses. One of the most fascinating is the activation of brown adipose tissue, or brown fat. Unlike white fat, which stores energy, brown fat burns calories to generate heat, increasing metabolic rate. Regular cold exposure enhances this process, improving insulin sensitivity and fat oxidation. For athletes, this means not only improved body composition but also greater metabolic efficiency during training and competition. Cold thermogenesis also trains vascular adaptability, as blood vessels learn to constrict and dilate with greater responsiveness, enhancing circulation across all conditions.

The combination of heat and cold exposure amplifies benefits through contrast protocols. Moving from sauna to ice bath, or alternating hot and cold immersion, creates a pumping effect on the vascular system. Blood vessels dilate in heat and constrict in cold, flushing waste products and drawing fresh oxygen and nutrients into tissues. Cardiovascular resilience improves, inflammation is moderated, and immune activity is stimulated. Many athletes incorporate contrast therapy after intense training or competition, not only to speed recovery but also to reinforce long-term adaptation. Beyond physiology, these practices cultivate mental toughness, as the ability to embrace discomfort becomes as valuable as the biological responses themselves.

Temperature manipulation is not about punishment but precision. Too much heat without hydration or recovery risks overstrain; too much cold without adaptation risks immune suppression. But when cycles of heat and cold are layered into training intelligently, they extend the boundaries of what the body can endure. Just as muscles grow from the alternating rhythm of stress and rest, the systems of thermoregulation, circulation, and metabolism grow from the alternating challenges of temperature extremes. The result is an organism more versatile, more efficient, and more resilient across the unpredictable conditions of both sport and life.

9.3 Natural Movement and Outdoor Training

Modern gyms provide control—air conditioning, standardized equipment, and predictable surfaces. Yet in the quest for control, much of the richness of movement has been lost. The human body evolved not under fluorescent lights and rubber floors but outdoors, negotiating irregular terrain, climbing obstacles, and adapting to ever-changing conditions. Reintroducing natural movement and outdoor training into modern practice reconnects the body to this heritage, developing not only strength and endurance but also coordination, balance, and awareness.

Obstacle-based training is one of the most effective ways to reawaken functional fitness. Climbing, crawling, jumping, and balancing require whole-body integration, demanding cooperation across muscle groups that isolation exercises rarely achieve. Navigating an obstacle course forces the body into dynamic problem solving, where no two movements are identical and adaptability is constantly tested. These challenges condition grip strength, core stability, and spatial awareness, building a kind of resilience that machines and fixed weights cannot replicate. Beyond physical benefits, obstacle training also engages the mind, requiring focus, creativity, and the ability to remain calm under pressure.

Trail running and hiking extend this principle into endurance practice. Unlike treadmill or track running, trails present constant variability—roots, rocks, slopes, and uneven ground. Each step demands proprioceptive refinement, as the body continually adjusts to maintain balance and momentum. This micro-adjustment strengthens stabilizing muscles in the ankles, knees, and hips, reducing injury risk and enhancing agility. Hiking adds another layer, blending endurance with strength as inclines challenge cardiovascular capacity while descents demand eccentric control. The combination creates a whole-body training effect rooted in natural environments, where fresh air, sunlight, and sensory richness amplify the benefits of physical exertion.

Beach and water training provide yet another dimension of environmental challenge. Sand destabilizes footing, forcing greater activation of stabilizing muscles and enhancing power transfer. Running on the beach, performing lunges in sand, or practicing plyometrics against its resistance develops lower-body strength while reducing joint impact. Water, with its resistance and buoyancy, creates a different stimulus altogether. Swimming builds cardiovascular endurance and upper-body power, while shallow-water sprints and resistance exercises challenge coordination and strength in low-impact conditions. Training in these environments not only diversifies adaptation but also cultivates resilience against fatigue by conditioning the body in settings where every movement feels unfamiliar.

Outdoor training carries psychological benefits that magnify physical ones. Exposure to natural light regulates circadian rhythms, improving sleep and hormonal balance. Contact with green and blue spaces—forests, mountains, oceans—reduces cortisol and enhances mood, creating a recovery effect even as training unfolds. Unlike indoor gyms, where distractions abound, outdoor training fosters presence, grounding attention in the immediate environment. Athletes who train outdoors often report greater enjoyment, reduced perceived effort, and improved consistency, making adherence as natural as the movements themselves.

Integrating natural movement and outdoor training does not mean abandoning the gym but complementing it. Strength machines and barbells provide controlled overload, while natural environments introduce variability and adaptability. Together, they build a body that is not only strong in measured lifts but also competent in unpredictable conditions. In this way, training becomes preparation not just for competition or aesthetics but for the real-world demands of life.

Environmental optimization, whether through temperature extremes or natural landscapes, reminds us that fitness is not confined to four walls. It is an ongoing dialogue with the forces of nature—heat, cold, air, water, terrain—that shaped human evolution. By embracing these forces instead of shielding ourselves from them, we rediscover a deeper resilience and expand the boundaries of what performance can mean.

Chapter 10: The Integration Protocol — Creating Your Personal Performance System

"The difference between good and great athletes isn't talent—it's the ability to integrate multiple performance systems into one seamless practice."

10.1 Building Your Performance Dashboard

The pursuit of peak fitness is often derailed not by lack of effort but by lack of integration. Many individuals excel at training hard, others at eating well, and still others at prioritizing sleep and recovery. Rarely are all these elements aligned in a coherent system. True performance emerges not from isolated excellence but from the ability to connect training, nutrition, recovery, and mindset into a feedback-driven framework that evolves with the individual. This is the essence of building a personal performance dashboard: creating a living system of metrics, feedback, and adjustments that transforms effort into measurable, sustainable progress.

A performance dashboard begins with clarity about what truly matters. In business, key performance indicators (KPIs) guide strategy; in fitness, the same principle applies. Rather than drowning in endless data points, the individual identifies a handful of markers that reflect training progress, nutritional alignment, and recovery quality. For training, this may involve tracking progression in compound lifts, improvements in sprint times, or endurance benchmarks. For nutrition, metrics might include macronutrient distribution, body composition changes, or post-meal glucose stability. For recovery, sleep quality, heart rate variability, and subjective readiness scores offer critical insight. The purpose is not to reduce the complexity of human performance into numbers alone but to select metrics that illuminate the connection between effort and adaptation.

Wearable technology has transformed this process. Devices that track heart rate variability, sleep cycles, step counts, and training loads now provide constant streams of data once reserved for laboratories. Integrated wisely, these tools become extensions of awareness, showing patterns invisible to intuition alone. A wearable might reveal that high-intensity training sessions performed late in the evening disrupt deep sleep, or that morning workouts coincide with higher readiness scores. Continuous glucose monitors can expose how specific foods spike or stabilize blood sugar, providing immediate feedback on nutritional choices. The key is not to become enslaved to devices but to use them as mirrors, reflecting back the body's state and guiding adjustments that improve efficiency.

Biomarker testing deepens this feedback by moving beyond external measures into the biochemical. Blood tests that assess vitamin D, testosterone, thyroid hormones, iron, and inflammation markers provide a snapshot of internal health. Saliva and urine testing offer insights into cortisol rhythms and hydration status. Periodic biomarker assessments reveal whether the external practices of training, eating, and sleeping are translating into internal optimization. For example, an athlete who trains diligently but shows chronically elevated cortisol may need to adjust recovery protocols. Another who eats a nutrient-rich diet but shows low magnesium may require targeted supplementation. These insights allow for precision rather than guesswork, making each intervention purposeful.

A dashboard without adjustment is static and quickly becomes irrelevant. This is where performance audits come into play. By reviewing metrics weekly, patterns emerge that inform strategy. Was strength progression slower during weeks of poor sleep? Did endurance improve when carbohydrate intake was timed more precisely around training? Did recovery markers improve during weeks of consistent meditation or nature exposure? These audits create feedback loops where actions are evaluated not in isolation but in terms of outcomes. Training becomes less about following a rigid plan and more about evolving with the body's responses.

Weekly audits also serve a psychological function. They create a structured moment of reflection where the athlete steps back from the noise of daily effort to see the bigger picture. Instead of being swept up in frustration over a single bad workout, one can recognize broader trends of progress. Instead of guessing whether nutrition is aligned, data confirms or challenges assumptions. This rhythm of reflection fosters consistency, as the individual knows that effort is being measured, reviewed, and adapted with intention. It transforms fitness from blind repetition into a process of continuous learning.

The strength of a performance dashboard lies in its integration. Training metrics without recovery markers risk overtraining. Recovery data without nutritional context may mislead. Nutrition without performance indicators may optimize health but fail to enhance output. Only by weaving these together into a holistic picture can the individual see the interplay of systems. For instance, noticing that high carbohydrate meals before intense sessions improve bar speed but disrupt sleep when eaten too late allows for strategic timing. Observing that deep sleep quality improves after mobility sessions but declines with evening screen use creates actionable changes. Each variable becomes part of a living web where adjustments in one area ripple across others.

This integration does not demand perfection but iteration. A dashboard is not a scorecard of failure but a map for refinement. It reveals when training intensity must be pulled back, when nutrition requires recalibration, when recovery practices need prioritization. Over time, the individual learns the language of their own body, no longer relying on generic advice but on personalized insights. This autonomy is the ultimate goal: the capacity to guide oneself through the complexities of performance with clarity and confidence.

For competitive athletes, the performance dashboard becomes a competitive edge. While talent and hard work set the foundation, the ability to integrate and adjust separates good from great. An athlete who notices dips in HRV two days before competition can proactively increase recovery efforts, arriving sharper than one who ignores the signals. A lifter who aligns biomarker improvements with performance peaks can structure training cycles more effectively. A runner who connects nutritional choices with glucose stability and endurance outcomes refines fueling to an art. Integration transforms randomness into precision.

For everyday individuals, the benefits are equally profound. Building a dashboard creates accountability and clarity, cutting through the confusion of endless fitness advice. It reveals whether efforts are aligned with goals, whether fatigue is the result of overtraining or poor sleep, whether nutritional struggles stem from timing or quality. It shifts the narrative from guessing to knowing, from frustration to empowerment.

The creation of a personal performance system, anchored by a dashboard, represents the culmination of fine fitness. It acknowledges that the body is complex but not unknowable, that effort matters but only when guided, that recovery and nutrition are not afterthoughts but coequal pillars with training. It transforms the pursuit of fitness from a fragmented endeavor into a unified practice where every action has context, every choice has consequence, and every outcome feeds back into the next cycle of growth.

In the end, building a performance dashboard is about integration—bringing together training, nutrition, recovery, and consciousness into one system of awareness and action. It is about making the invisible visible, turning the body's subtle signals into clear feedback, and transforming feedback into strategy. It is the tool that ensures talent is maximized, effort is rewarded, and potential is not wasted. The difference between good and great is not found in genetics alone but in this ability to integrate, to create a system where the art of performance becomes a science of precision and adaptation.

10.2 The 90-Day Transformation Framework

Change is most effective when it is time-bound. Long enough to create meaningful adaptation, yet short enough to maintain urgency, a ninety-day window offers the perfect balance between aspiration and action. Within three months, the body can remodel muscle, shift metabolic pathways, establish new sleep rhythms, and rewire habits. The ninety-day framework transforms fitness from vague ambition into a structured process of measurable outcomes, sustainable behaviors, and consistent reinforcement.

The first step in such a framework is the design of phase-specific goals. Rather than chasing everything at once, focus narrows to one or two outcomes that align with the broader vision of performance. A strength-focused ninety days might prioritize measurable increases in compound lifts, while an endurance block could target improved times across set distances. Each phase includes clear markers to evaluate progress—numbers on the bar, distances covered, energy levels maintained—so that achievement is tangible. These markers do more than record progress; they provide feedback that guides adjustments, ensuring momentum continues rather than stalls.

Yet numbers alone are not transformation. Sustainable change emerges from daily behaviors that accumulate into new identities. Habit stacking provides the mechanism for this shift. By linking a new behavior to an established one, the brain builds bridges of consistency. Drinking a protein shake immediately after brushing teeth in the morning, performing mobility work right after the last email of the day, or practicing box breathing before turning off the lights—these small connections transform willpower into automation. Over ninety days, the repetition of stacked habits redefines routines, embedding performance-enhancing practices into the fabric of daily life.

Consistency, however, is the greatest challenge in transformation. Implementation intentions offer a solution by moving from vague goals to specific plans: "If situation X arises, then I will do Y." Instead of aspiring to eat better, one decides, "If I eat out, I will choose a protein-centered option before considering sides." Instead of promising to train more, one decides, "If it is Tuesday at 7 a.m., I will begin my workout regardless of mood." These intentions reduce friction by eliminating indecision, replacing it with predetermined actions. Environmental design complements this strategy, shaping surroundings so that success is the path of least resistance. Laying out workout clothes the night before, stocking the fridge with ready-to-eat vegetables, or silencing notifications during evening hours creates an ecosystem where desired behaviors happen naturally.

The ninety-day framework is not only about intensity but sustainability. Each block ends with reflection: what worked, what struggled, what needs recalibration. The lessons of one cycle inform the next, creating a rhythm of growth and consolidation. Over time, these three-month arcs accumulate, each contributing to a larger narrative of transformation. The body adapts, the mind strengthens, and behaviors become identity. Fitness is no longer something one does but something one lives.

10.3 Long-Term Athletic Development and Longevity

If the ninety-day framework provides urgency, long-term athletic development offers perspective. Fitness is not a sprint but a lifelong practice, and progress must be framed across years and even decades. The concept of training age—the number of years an individual has trained with consistency and progression—becomes a guide for how programs evolve over time. A beginner may progress rapidly with simple linear increases, but as training age advances, adaptations require more nuanced programming, greater emphasis on recovery, and deeper integration of lifestyle. Viewing fitness through this lens prevents impatience, recognizing that mastery unfolds across seasons, not weeks.

Longevity requires more than progression; it demands resilience. Injury prevention is central to sustaining performance, for a sidelined athlete cannot adapt. Movement screening provides the foundation, identifying asymmetries, weaknesses, or restrictions before they manifest as breakdowns. A limited range of motion in the hips may predict lower back strain; unstable shoulders may foreshadow rotator cuff issues. Addressing these risks proactively through corrective exercises, mobility flows, and load management ensures that progress is not derailed. Injury prevention is not reactive therapy but proactive design, embedding resilience into the very structure of training.

Long-term development also means evolving goals as life stages change. The ambitions of a twenty-year-old striving for peak power differ from those of a forty-year-old balancing performance with career and family, or a sixty-year-old seeking to maintain vitality and independence. Legacy fitness goals acknowledge this evolution, creating benchmarks that transcend temporary numbers. For some, it may be the ability to play sports with grandchildren without fatigue. For others, it may be completing marathons into later decades, maintaining strength to travel freely, or simply sustaining energy and mental clarity into old age. These goals align fitness not only with performance but with meaning, ensuring that training supports life rather than consuming it.

The blueprint for long-term athletic development integrates all dimensions of fine fitness. It uses short-term cycles like the ninety-day framework to drive adaptation, while anchoring those cycles in a decade-long trajectory. It embraces progression but tempers it with patience, pushing when the body is ready, recovering when it demands rest. It builds resilience not only through strength and endurance but through mobility, awareness, and hormonal balance. Most importantly, it grounds fitness in purpose—aligning every rep, every meal, every night of sleep with a vision of a life lived fully and energetically.

Longevity is not passive preservation but active cultivation. It is the recognition that aging is not merely the decline of capacity but the opportunity to refine it, to adapt training and lifestyle in ways that extend vitality. By focusing on prevention, integration, and evolution, long-term athletic development ensures that the pursuit of performance is not abandoned with age but transformed into a lifelong practice.

Conclusion — The Harmony of Body, Fuel, and Flow

The journey through fine fitness has been a journey of integration. Each chapter has peeled back a layer of the human system, showing that strength, resilience, and vitality do not emerge from isolated practices but from the weaving together of body, fuel, and flow into one coherent whole. Training shapes the body, but without recovery it is wasted. Nutrition fuels every adaptation, but without movement its potential lies dormant. Awareness channels focus and flow, but without physiological readiness it cannot reach its full expression. The great secret of performance is not in extremes but in harmony.

What makes this convergence powerful is not complexity but coherence. When the body is challenged with intelligence, when nutrition is timed and composed with precision, and when consciousness is cultivated to remain present in movement, the systems of human performance amplify one another. Hormones shift into balance, mitochondria multiply, neural pathways refine, and the immune system strengthens. Fitness ceases to be about chasing numbers or appearances and becomes the art of creating a life where every action resonates with vitality.

Integration is not static but dynamic. Life changes, environments shift, and goals evolve. The practices outlined here are not rigid prescriptions but principles that adapt with the individual. A young athlete may apply them to chase peak performance, while a professional may use them to sustain clarity and energy in demanding careers. A parent may embrace them to maintain resilience through long days, and an elder may use them to preserve independence and vitality. The convergence of body, fuel, and flow does not belong to one stage of life or one type of person—it belongs to anyone who chooses to live with intention.

Perhaps the most liberating truth is that fine fitness is not about perfection. There will be missed sessions, meals that fall short, nights of poor sleep, and days where focus scatters. What matters is not flawless execution but returning to the system, recalibrating, and continuing forward. The body is forgiving when treated with consistency, the mind is trainable when given patience, and fuel is always available to be refined. The strength of this approach lies in its resilience, in its ability to absorb setbacks and still move toward long-term transformation.

In embracing the convergence, fitness becomes more than a pursuit—it becomes a way of being. Every breath, every step, every meal, every moment of awareness contributes to a larger rhythm. Training is no longer confined to the gym; it is present in the way we walk, sit, breathe, and recover. Nutrition is no longer an abstract calculation; it is the daily act of providing the body with the tools to thrive. Flow is no longer a rare accident; it is a state we can invite and practice, a bridge between effort and artistry.

The promise of fine fitness is not simply more muscle, less fat, or better numbers on a stopwatch. It is the promise of living fully in the body you inhabit, of experiencing clarity of mind, steadiness of energy, and joy in movement. It is about cultivating strength that protects, endurance that sustains, and awareness that enriches. It is about building not just a body but a life that is resilient, adaptable, and alive.

As you close this book, the invitation is simple: begin to integrate. Take what you have learned about training, recovery, nutrition, and flow, and weave them into your daily practice. Do not aim to implement everything at once. Instead, align small actions with the larger vision of balance. Over time, those small actions will compound into transformation, and transformation will evolve into mastery.

Fine fitness is not the end of a journey but the beginning of one that continues for as long as you breathe. Every day offers a chance to align body, fuel, and flow more closely, to refine the art of living with vitality. In this convergence lies the true essence of human potential—not fragmented, not forced, but harmonious. And in that harmony, performance and life itself reach their highest expression.

www.ingramcontent.com/pod-product-compliance
Lightning Source LLC
Chambersburg PA
CBHW070740230426
43669CB00014B/2522